Wicked (Really Wicked!) Reviews

"Even though I'm not Catholic, the Pope should make me a Saint for staying married to him for 47 years. It's taken a miracle." – *Linda Hocutt, wife*

"It's a good thing you don't need a job, because no one would hire you after reading this." – *Jana Hocutt Lacroix, daughter*

"Have you got rocks for brains?" – *Daphne Hocutt Slife, daughter*

"Better than Lunesta. And it's non-addictive." – *Mike Hocutt, brother*

"TOO MANY WORDS!!!" – *Sarah (the Driver) Hocutt, sister-in-law*

"What happened to your side of the family to cause this? I hope it's not hereditary!" – *Savannah Slife, granddaughter*

"You're proof mom was right about all those concussions." – *Jacob Slife, grandson*

"He introduced me to root beer and buys me ice cream. I'll remember the good times and try to forget this ever happened." – *Bailey Lacroix, granddaughter*

"I don't know what this is all about. All I want to do is run and jump." – *Lily Lacroix, granddaughter*

"I never really knew Uncle Jerry. I owe you one dad." – *Scott Hocutt, nephew*

"I've got nothing. (Dad always said that if you can't say something nice about someone, then say nothing.)" – *Diana Hocutt Nungesser, niece*

"Screw the review! Ask him where he left me and Linda stranded in Windsor, Canada. The creep!" – *Jo Anne Hocutt Bennett, sister*

"Bad boy! Bad boy!" – *Banjo, granddog*

Wickedly Quick Look Inside

Read it for laughs.

butt-dial, *v*. Smart ass.

consciously incompetent, *adj*. The second lowest level of competence. You're stupid and you know it. Why the *Dummies* and *Idiots* books are so popular.

good enough. After recovering from the shock of seeing the recent college tuition hikes, what you tell your new high school grad about his education.

no, *adv*. Final decision not in your favor. It doesn't mean, "Maybe. Why don't you try again?"
  "How can I say 'No' to you – and yet I have." – *Nora Ephron*

puppy dog close, *n*. A sales technique that puts the product in the prospect's hands for a trial period to show friends and family and to instill feelings of ownership, while at the same time creating guilt for wanting to return it. Like what hospitals do with mothers of newborns.

texting, *v*. Wrds wtht vwls. (Why texting isn't big in Hawaii.)
  "Dear Students: I know when you're texting in class. Seriously, no one just looks down at their crotch and smiles. Sincerely, Your Teacher." – *Sign posted in high school class*

unconsciously incompetent, *n*. The lowest level of competence. You're stupid and you don't know it. It's when someone asks you to name the ten Supreme Court Justices and you actually come up with ten names.

unintended consequences. Didn't see that coming! Your mind leaving you thoughtless and alone without telling you it was going.

"Oops!" – *Embarrassed presidential contender, and Texas Governor, Rick Perry with his 53-second brain freeze unable to remember one of the three federal departments he wanted to abolish in a nationally televised GOP debate*

Read it for business ideas.

cheese technique, *n*. A baited trap used by the salesperson to get to first base with a prospect who refuses to consider changing vendors.

"We send a copy of the book *Who Moved My Cheese* to the buyer with this note: 'This only takes one hour to read. It talks about the importance of change. I'll call next week to see what you think.'" – *Dallas saleswoman**

dead fish handshake, *n*. The quickest way to be shown the door on a job interview. The most misunderstood handshake in America because it's interpreted as a sign of weakness. It's not. It means that person probably works with their hands for a living (doctor, dentist, nurse); has a sport or hobby where they use their hands (golf, knitting, musician); or has a physical challenge and can't give a firm handshake.

"If an applicant for a sales position gives me the dead fish handshake, I rule them out (snapping her fingers) just like that!" – *Sales manager for a Silicon Valley tech firm**

dress code, *n*. Standard of dress expected by businesses. How you dress affects your attitude and how others react to you. Wear an orange jumpsuit to the mall with D.O.C. stenciled on the back and see the reactions you get.

"He's still recovering from injuries he suffered when he went to a costume party dressed as a piñata." – *Unknown*

Driver personality, *n*. Someone with a dominant, pushy, impatient attitude. Big picture people. Talk to them in bulleted points – not in complete sentences. All correspondence should fit on a Post-It note.

Hershey kiss technique, *n*. Send an infant's shoe with a Hershey kiss inside to your prospect with this note: "It would be sweet to get my foot in the door."

"I sent fifteen shoes to my prospects the week after your seminar and got five appointments from them the following week."
– *Testimonial from the owner of a print shop in New Jersey**

telephone cold call, *n*. Outgoing calls made by a telemarketer, inside salesperson, or outside salesperson. One call every thirty minutes of each working day (244 working days per year) adds up to over 3800 cold calls in a year. Now try convincing your boss you don't have the time to cold call.

Read it for inspiration.

believers, *n.pl*. Completely persuaded. Leaders. People with a purpose. What bosses want a team of. SEALs, Special Forces, Rangers.

"Rangers lead the way." – *Army Ranger motto*
"The only easy day was yesterday." – *Navy SEAL motto*

commitment, *n*. Belief gives you hope. Commitment compels you to find a way. It's burning your ships on the enemy's foreign shore with no escape, leaving only one of two possible outcomes.

guru, *n*. There are no gurus with life's answers. Look for people who will ask you the tough questions so you can find your own answers.

"You don't seem to be happy in your job here. If you could do anything in the world – anything – what would you really want to do with your life?" – *Business owner to employee who quickly found his calling, quit his job, and started his own successful business**

impossible, *adj*. That's what I do.
 "Why not you?" – *Seattle Seahawk's quarterback Russell Wilson's dad's advice to him as a youngster; and what he challenged his teammates with "Why not us?" as he led his team to win Super Bowl XLVIII in just his second year (and the most-watched television event in U.S. history, February 2, 2014)*

learn, *v*. To finally understand, either voluntarily or involuntarily.
 "We're going to operate a certain way, and if you're not, we're not changing our standard for your actions." – *University of Washington football coach Chris Petersen on how he handles discipline with his players*

silence, *n*. When words won't do.
 "Silence can be so loud." – *James Lee Burke*

want, *v*. Bosses want people who *want* to do what others avoid doing and have the attitude that "We can do more, and we can do better."
 "I can't want it for him." – *Seattle Mariners manager on returning player who showed up for spring practice forty pounds over target weight, showed no desire to participate in offseason conditioning, and was in jeopardy of losing his job*

The Wickedly Fun Dictionary of Business

Words That Escaped Me Before My Brain Finished Downloading

Jerry Hocutt

Chugwater Publishing

Seattle, Washington

The Wickedly Fun Dictionary of Business – Words That Escaped Me Before My Brain Finished Downloading © 2014 Jerry E. Hocutt, Jr. Printed and bound in the United States of America. All rights reserved. No part of this book may be reproduced or transmitted in any form or by any means, electronic or mechanical, including photocopying, recording, or by an information storage and retrieval system – except by a reviewer who may quote brief passages in a review to be printed in a magazine, newspaper, or on the Web – without permission in writing from the publisher. For information contact Jerry Hocutt, Hocutt & Associates, Inc., 24933 – 132nd Place S.E., Kent, WA 98042. First edition.

Although the author and publisher have made every effort to ensure the accuracy and completeness of information contained in this book, and tried to correctly attribute all quotes to their sources, we assume no responsibility for errors, inaccuracies, omissions, or any inconsistency herein. Any slights of people, places, or organizations are unintentional.

First printing 2014

Hocutt, Jerry
 The Wickedly Fun Dictionary of Business – Words That Escaped Me Before My Brain Finished Downloading
1st edition.

ISBN 978-0-615-95254-3
Library of Congress Control Number 2014900991
 1. Business. 2. Sales. 3. Dictionary. 4. Humor. 5. Marketing.
 6. Management. II. Hocutt, Jr., Jerry E. III. Title

Cold Calling for Cowards® is a registered trademark of Hocutt & Associates, Inc.

Cover design by Jana Hocutt Lacroix

Wicked Referrals – If You'd Rather Not Cold Call

Attention business owners, sales managers, salespeople, and marketing executives: see the Appendix for how to get a PDF abridged edition of *The Wickedly Fun Dictionary of Business* to use as a wicked referral strategy. Put your exclusive one-page advertisement in it and give it away free to anyone you like.

Linda – words are not enough

preface, *n.* I wrote this because...

   a. It's quick, quirky, and fun.
   b. It's inspirational, educational, and entertaining.
   c. I live for the suffering and bleeding through every pore in my body that writing brings to my day.

There Is No Downside to Having Fun

People like to have fun and they want to be around those who are fun. Fun doesn't care about age, sex, title, income, education, successes, health, religion, or nationality. Fun is networking with strangers or closing a new deal. It's meditating alone on the beach or screaming your lungs out in a stadium filled with 65,000 of your closest rabid friends. Fun is watching your kids play at the park or jogging on the trail with your dog. Fun is, well, just fun.

The Wickedly Fun Dictionary of Business was conceived from my programs, "You'll Always Be Happy If You're Having Fun – How to Have Fun Doing (Almost) Anything" and "What Bosses Want: True Believers".

> **fun**, *n*. A good experience. Something you not only *like* to do, but *want* to do because of the challenge, excitement, or entertainment. The more fun you have, the more you do. The more you do, the quicker you learn. The quicker you learn, the better you get. An unexpected bonus: you're never discouraged when you're having fun.

This book uses humor to share lessons about business, life, and beliefs because humor is the truth sneaking up on tiptoes. But I've included some definitions that are plain silly just for the fun of it. Think of them as the Krispy Kremes you would sneak into the nutritional food group.

Russell Wilson, Seattle's Super Bowl XLVIII quarterback, said his belief in *impossible* contributed to helping the Seahawks win their first ever championship in only his second year in the league. *Appointment* has a startling discovery by a Milwaukee salesman that shows why you may not get invited back for that second interview. *Book* has a business owner's question that could save you wasted hours in the job interviewing process. *Details* has a life lesson from the chairman of Zales that shows regardless of your experience and education, if you do this one thing you will have an edge on 95% of those you're competing against.

Why a dictionary? Words fascinate me, and definitions require simplicity and clarity. Words can take on many different meanings depending upon the situations they're used in, who's saying them, and how they're being said. Words can hide the truth by telling a lie, or expose a lie by telling the truth. Books have been written trying to explain even a single word: hope, fear, faith, happiness, wisdom, mindfulness, love, prayer. Accounting.

Here's what psychologists say about men, women, and words: men are stingy with their words and strive to be specific with the ones they choose. Women not so much. Men take words literally. Women don't. Men cut to the chase. Women – tell me more. Men favor detached, unemotional words. Just the facts, ma'am. Women use words to plumb the depths of their feelings. Ewww!

The Wickedly Fun Dictionary of Business is a G-rated quick read, fun and funny (somewhat), and educational and inspiring. It's a hand lifting the veil from the words we use to reveal the thoughts we don't want others to see.

You don't need to read the book from cover to cover. When you need a diversion, when you need a laugh, when you're looking for a business idea, open it to any page and surprise yourself with what you find. There are over 1200 definitions and over 600 business ideas and inspirational quotes.

There's something for everyone, whether you own or work for a business, whether you're in sales or service, or whether you're looking for work or travel for work.

When you see an asterisk in a comment after the definition, that's something that happened to me personally or I have firsthand knowledge about.

* * *

If you're a business owner, sales manager, salesperson, or marketing executive, there's a surprising referral strategy for you in the Appendix if you'd rather not cold call to find new business.

Jerry Hocutt

Contents

Words	1-219
Appendix – Referral Strategy	i
About the Author	ii
Speaker	iii
Titles by Jerry Hocutt	iv

a wing and a prayer. The first and last items on the pilot's pre-flight checklist.

"We're glad you're flying with us today folks. We should be arriving in San Jose in three hours and forty minutes. (Long pause.) Sorry about that. Make that Phoenix." – *Pilot after being corrected by First Officer of real destination before leaving gate**

acceptance of offer. The last step to create a binding contract. It's the "I do's" to the wedding vows.

"Tour guide: 'I'm sorry Mr. Holland, but we left your new bride behind at the hotel.' Mr. Holland: 'Thank goodness. I thought I was going deaf.'" – *Unknown*

accounts payable, *n*. That line's busy. The customer's department you call to get payment on an overdue invoice. The department consists of only a voicemail recording that is always full so you can't leave a message.

accounts receivable, *n*. The department that answers every call on the first ring because they want their money. If you try to trick them into transferring you to accounts payable their response is, "They're not in. I'll send you to their voicemail."

Achilles' heel, *n*. A company's weak link. Usually their employees' attitudes.

"60% of customers stop coming to a place of business because of a negative attitude or indifference towards them by employees." – *U.S. News & World Report*

acid test, *n*. Can the salesperson cold call? Does the employee's history indicate she can handle the pressure if she's promoted? Does the job applicant have the passion for our type of work?

"Part of our job interview process is to send the sales applicant out into the field with one of our salespeople making cold calls. You'd be surprised how many decide sales isn't for them. And it saves us a lot of time and money in the interviewing and hiring process." – *Fortune 1000 branch manager**

across-the-board, *adj*. An action that affects (almost) everyone equally. "We all have to tighten our belts and cut our budgets by 10%," warned the hedge fund manager on his conference call. He then left to deposit his $21 million annual bonus.

"Goldman Sachs slashes 900 jobs, awards CEO $26 million in 2012" – *Bloomberg News, June 2013*

action plan, *n*. A salesperson's "how to" plan to reach his sales goals: do this, get that. The plan fails because there is no "do".

"It doesn't matter what I believe, but what I do." – *Jackie Robinson*

active listening, *n*. Pretending to listen while asking questions. But the questions are designed to lead the customer to the conclusion the questioner wants. Like three-card monte.

adapt, *v*. Changes you have to make to keep your job, like it or not. Like evolution, you really have no choice, that's the way it is.

"Nobody told me how hard and lonely change is." – *Joan Gilbertson*

add-on sale, *n*. Additional purchase made by an existing customer that the comptroller doesn't think salespeople should be paid a full commission for because "that wasn't really selling."

adjustment, *n*. What airplanes and ships must do when they find they're off course. Same for companies and workers. Not always easy, but always necessary.

"You usually can't change your behavior by simply resolving to do something. If that were true, New Year's resolutions would actually work. Knowing what to do is not the same as being able to do it. If that were true, people would find it easier to lose weight." – *David Brooks*

advantage, *n*. To be in a superior position to make the other person sweat. "Your competitor took me to lunch yesterday and made quite an offer. I'm seriously considering it."

"Boxing has an advantage over politics. In the ring, you know exactly what your opponent's intentions are." – *Eder Jofre*

adversity, *n*. Infinite growth experiences that come at inopportune times.

"There is no education like adversity." – *Benjamin Disraeli*

advertise, *v*. Used to market goods and services hoping it will find so many customers that you won't have to cold call. It won't.

"It certainly pays to advertise – there are twenty-six mountains in Colorado that are higher than Pike's Peak." – *Unknown*

advertisement, *n*. Political ads are fast replacing automobile ads since politicians can now be bought and sold year-round while having multiple owners.

"There's no background check for buying a senator." – *David Letterman*

advertising, *v*. Baiting the hook to see if you'll get any bites.

advertising agency, *n*. A marketing group that thinks (knows?) consumers are idiots.

"Don't tell my mother I work in an advertising agency – she thinks I play piano in a whorehouse." – *Jacques Seguela*

advertising message, *n*. The less said the better.

"I have always believed that writing advertisements is the second most profitable form of writing. The first, of course, is ransom notes." – *Philip Dusenberry*

advice, *n*. Gratis criticisms you didn't ask for, certainly won't pay for, and definitely won't take.

"If it's free, it's advice; if you pay for it, it's counseling; if you can use either one, it's a miracle." – *Jack Adams*

advocate, *n*. The customer's salesperson who must serve as their intermediary with management, service, and billing. How salespeople build customer loyalty, and why companies lose business when their salespeople leave.

"We never thought we'd lose 1000 of your 1500 accounts within the first year after you left." – *General manager lamenting to former salesman**

aggressive, *adj*. A pit bull attitude. But not everyone likes pit bulls.

"I love our salesman because he's like a pit bull: he won't give up and he won't take 'no' for an answer. But his sales suck. Our customers and prospects tell me they don't like his attitude and refuse to do business with him. And his co-workers can't stand him. What should I do?" – *Baltimore business owner**

aghast, *adj*. Shocked; struck with terror. The look on the face of the firm's advertising rep when she was shown she misplaced the decimal point on the full page ad for the product's price of $1499 to read $14.99. On the plus side, the orders are rolling in.

"United Airlines accidentally posts $0 to $10 fares. Passengers reported buying tickets for $5 to $10 before United shut down the bookings." – *AP (September 12, 2013)*

agree, *v.* Time to zip it. Many sales are lost because the salesperson just can't shut up.

"When the other person nods his head affirmatively but says nothing, it's time to stop talking." – *Henry Haskins*

air marshals, *n.pl.* Guns on a plane.

air quotes, *n.* Sarcastic, irritating finger quotes that are meant to show, ironically, sarcasm. We get it. Stop it.

airplane, *n.* The second inconvenience at the end of the first – the TSA grab and grope line. The only difference between an airplane and a cattle truck is that the cattle don't have to pay.

"I don't think they understand how little of the airplane arrived with them." – *John Nance, national aviation expert and pilot, commenting on the pilots of the crashed Asiana Airlines Boeing 777, flight 214, in July 2013, who delayed for 90 seconds in ordering the evacuation of the plane, thinking the landing "wasn't that bad". The plane arrived without its tail section (left in San Francisco bay at the end of the runway), two flight attendants ejected from the now absent tail section area, doing a belly flop and then thrown into the air balancing on one wing while making an acrobatic 360 degree rotation. Its landing gear was strewn over the runway, both engines ripped from the wings, cabin seats pulled from their anchors, and coming to rest in the field off the runway, with the cabin filling with smoke, leaking fuel, on fire, and with over 180 injured and three dead.*

airport, *n.* Where voyeurs go to watch government enforced strip searches. No parking or waiting at curbside. Cars will be ticketed and towed. Move along now.

"I spend all my time traveling, but I never arrive anywhere."
– *Henning Mankell*

alarming, *adj*. Receiving an unexpected text from your best customer: "Call ASAP!!!" You assume it's bad news. But it could be great news! Naw, it's not. Just kidding.

"Commencement speaker's dilemma: How can I tell the graduates that the future is in their hands without alarming the rest of the audience?" – *Unknown*

all-in, *n*. Let's go! Total commitment without reservation. Also, the last call for the clown car.

aloof, *n*. Emotionally not there, like when tech support is going on and on and on about why your computer is on the fritz.

alternate close, *n*. An "either/or" sales trap that makes the customer feel like she's in control because she can choose between two answers (both of which favor the salesperson). It's when the warden asks the condemned, "Electric or lethal injection?"

ambiguity, *n*. A word with multiple meanings, depending upon who's doing the interpreting. To the salesperson, "customer" is a commission; to the service person, the customer is a pain in the neck; to the comptroller, the customer is just another number.

"Keep in mind...to a dog you are family, to a cat you are staff." – *Unknown*

ambitious, *adj*. A trait desired in all employees until they start having better ideas than the boss.

"A genius knows the answer before there is a question." – *Robert Oppenheimer*

Amiable personality, *n*. Not a boat rocker. The Boy Scout or Girl Scout of the personalities: loyal, trustworthy, obedient, friendly, thrifty, brave, reverent. Need others to help them make decisions. Intimidated by the Driver personalities. Favorite song: Kumbaya. Favorite food: comfort. 35% of the population. Must engage in small talk before they will begin to trust you. (Cf. *Analytical, Expressive, and Driver personalities*.)

amortization, *n*. Writing an asset off as a loss. What venture capitalists do to workers they layoff when they raid and pillage their company.

analogy, *n*. Comparison involving unrelated objects to show familial DNA.
    "The GOP is a Mad Men party in a Modern Family world." – *Matthew Dowd*

Analytical personality, *n*. People who use too many words. Can make decisions, but won't until the eleventh hour. Takes five to seven contacts before they'll even think of making a decision to move to the next step. Never have enough information. Love to tell you what they know and what they think. Can't stand the Expressive personalities because they're "nothing but a bunch of showboaters". 35% of people. Make good salespeople because they have the patience, get the facts, and follow-up. Have a dry sense of humor as prickly as a West Texas barbed wire fence. (Cf. *Amiable, Driver, and Expressive personalities*.)

analyze, *v.t*. Let me think about it.
    "Focus on making the correct decisions at the poker table and not the outcome." – *Daniel Negreanu*

anger, *n*. There's a time and place for it. Plants the seed for necessary changes that otherwise would not have been considered. "I can't believe they're treating us like that! Find another vendor."
    "'Why aren't you angry?' the interviewer asked. 'I would be if I thought it would help.'" – *Nelson Mandela*

annoy, *v.* In-laws, know-it-alls, and kids on a road trip.

"The reason the Obama campaign was so successful in raising such huge campaign funds by constantly sending out those irritating emails is because their 'nerds' were taught to 'get over the fear of being annoying.'" – *New York Times*

anxiety, *n.* Nervous anticipation that what you want to happen won't. Why you can't get back to sleep after waking at two in the morning.

"We don't get what we want, we get what we expect." – *C. James Jensen*

apologize, *v.i.* What women look for men to do. That's not happening.

"When we are in the supermarket and someone rams our ankle with a shopping cart then apologizes for doing so, why do we say, 'It's all right.'? Well, it isn't all right so why don't we say, 'That hurt, you stupid idiot!'?" – *Unknown*

apology, *n.* I was wrong?

"I'm sorry. I didn't know that was your area. But it's okay if I keep the sale, isn't it?" – *Saleswoman caught poaching customers in another's territory**

application, *n.* How the customer will put your product to use. Sometimes it's best not to ask why, so you'll have a legal defense.

"I need the surveillance equipment installed discreetly in my husband's office without his knowledge." – *Wife to security consultant*

appointment, *n.* A client's meeting to see if there is a future with the salesperson. First appointments are easier to get than the second because the salesperson has been eliminated on the first through various behaviors, statements, and findings. Most decision makers make up their minds within the first fifteen minutes.

"I asked the CEO why she wouldn't make a second appointment with me. 'Because of the way you shook my hand when you came in. You turned your palm down, forcing my palm up, making me submissive. You didn't do that with my three male vice presidents. I felt you were putting me down. I didn't like it.'" – *Milwaukee salesman who said he never knew he shook hands differently with women than with men, and why he never got in to that account again**

approval, *n*. Not required if it's the right thing to do.

approved, *v*. Blessed and cursed at the same time. "The customer approved the price without blinking an eye. We must have screwed something up."

armchair quarterback, *n*. The critic who didn't suit up for fear of getting sacked. "If it was me, I wouldn't have done it that way." Well it wasn't you, you stayed on the bench, and it's done.

arrogance, *n*. A spoiled, strutting heiress suffering from the delusion that she's responsible for her family's great wealth. Or, it could be your cat turning up his nose at the food in his dish.

ask, *v*. What sales managers want their salespeople to do to close the deal. What salespeople are reluctant to do saying, "I didn't think the time was right." The time never is right. Ask anyway.

"People don't want you to think you're entitled to their business – they want you to ask for it." – *Unknown*

assert, *v.t*. A forceful statement to influence others. The best thing a salesperson can say about her product is, "I own one too."

assertive, *n*. Aggressiveness without being ugly about it.

asset, *n*. An item of value: equipment, building, real estate. Assets can appreciate or depreciate. If they depreciate, like electronics, they can be written off. So can some staff when they lose their value.

assistant, *n*. The decision maker's wingman.
 "The difference between an assistant coach and the head coach is the difference between making a suggestion and making a decision." – *Bobby Knight*

attorney, *n*. What lawyers prefer to be called instead of ambulance chasers.
 "Are you taking singing lessons? Who's your teacher? Do you have a lawyer? Get a lawyer to sue her." – *Simon Cowell*

attrition, *n*. A culling of the weak and the old from the work herd. Man-eating crocs do the same thing on the banks of the Nile.

au pair, *n*. A mommy intern with an a foreign accent. Oui, oui.

audience, *n*. Where you sit if you're not a speaker at your national convention. Remember, the speaker is looking at you as being naked in order to calm his nerves. Try not to blush.
 "Always make the audience suffer as much as possible." – *Alfred Hitchcock*

audition, *n*. Job interview; sales interview. They can hire you or they can fire you.
 "It's so frustrating! I never can land a second interview. No one ever calls back. They're expecting me to sell myself on why I'd be a good salesperson and I can't do it." – *Recent college grad in Chicago interviewing for her first sales job**

authority, *n*. The unknown person who said you could do it, but who won't get in as much trouble as you're about to be in.

"I got permission from management to do it." – *Former Washington state employee who gave massages to co-workers at work to get the necessary hours to earn a masseuse license, and is being sued by the state**

awards, *n. pl.* The value of an award is not the recognition and accolades you get for having earned it. The value is in what you did, who you helped, and who you became to get it. This is true whether it's the merit badges you earned in the scouts, the company's employee of the month plaque, the hospital's volunteer of the year award, a Super Bowl ring, or the Congressional Medal of Honor.

B

B.S., *n*. Stinkin' lies and fabrications you don't want to step in.

background check, *n*. Performed by HR and the hiring manager to make sure no loaded loose cannons are put onto the payroll. Interviews give applicants a chance to explain their social media pics and postings. Then calls are made to former employers and friends. By the time background checks are completed the applicant has found another job.

"I asked the job applicant why he went to college. His ill-conceived answer: 'To party and socialize.'" – *AP*

back-room deal, *n*. Where shady agreements are reached out of sight of prying eyes. Normal routine business practices employed by the wealthy who think money solves everything and who don't accept "no" as an answer. When rookies are caught making such nefarious deals they admit it with, "I made a mistake I regret."

"It would have been more honest if he had said, 'I made a mistake that became public because I don't have enough practice at this.'" – *Seattle Times on pro basketball investor caught making illegal contributions to Sacramento's petition campaign to stop the King's arena momentum*

backstabbers, *n.pl.* Political gamesmanship and intrigue where the stabber gets to advance his cause without the irritating stabee being in a position to defend herself. Much backstabbing is found on social media where the perpetrator, when caught red-handed, pleads "mea culpa" (my bad) and gives a forced, false apology, only to take a stab at it again later.

"As a general rule, I abstain from reading the reports of attacks upon myself, wishing not to be provoked by that to which I cannot properly offer an answer." – *Abraham Lincoln*

backstory, *n.* How the customer came up with the idea for her business, pulled herself up by the bootstraps, and got to where she is today. A good salesperson seeks out the backstory because it establishes the main characters, shows how decisions are made, and identifies the company's objectives.

"I started these 5x5 soccer tournaments for the sixteenth and seventeenth players on the bench who never get to play; so now everyone gets to play. The games are lightning fast, exciting, and fun for players and fans alike with different themes and music each year." – *Founder of Yakima's Yak Attack that draws over 230 teams from four states**

backup plan, *n.* It's when you learn you may have to compromise.

"You'll be issued parachutes and must keep them on during the mission in case the plane should go down." – *Air Force captain of C-130 search and rescue flight to ride-alongs flying over the South China Sea**

bad advice, *n.* What seemed good at the time.

"Bad Advice $1" – *Handmade cardboard sign held by homeless man in Times Square**

badass, *adj*. Not you.
"Your name is not Calvin Klein. You're not an underwear model. If you want service here, pull up your pants." – *Sign on door at donut shop*

baggage check, *n*. Where you hastily remove three pounds of clothes from your suitcase to get in under the limit.

baggage claim, *n*. Where departing passengers are directed to go to place wagers on who's showed up.

bagman, *n*. The female Senator's intern.
"When Kay Bailey Hutchison represented Texas in the Senate, she had her purse trotted through the Capitol by a rotating cadre of young male aides, to some raised eyebrows. But now some version of the so-called 'purse boy' is almost commonplace." – *New York Times*

bait and switch, *n*. A résumé.

barring complications. Things are going fine. Keep your mouth shut.

barter, *v*. To trade services or products in lieu of cash. The one who initiates the trade has a product of less value than the product he wants from you. "I'll trade you a carton of Golden Carpet Clean for a two week stay in your Maui condo."

basics, *n*. The basics are the basics because they work.
"Excellence is achieved by mastery of the fundamentals." – *Vince Lombardi*

basketball technique, *n*. A marketing slam dunk that gets prospects to not only save your message, but guarantees it goes viral.

"My competitor sent basketballs to twenty-five of my customers with the inscription: 'Just wanted to bounce off a few ideas with you.' I lost five of my customers within a month." – *Chicago business owner**

bean counter, *n*. A numbers masseuse.

"A person decides to be an accountant when he discovers he doesn't have the charisma to be an undertaker." – *Unknown*

because, *conj*. Harvard's Dr. Ellen Langer says this one word gets people to do or to accept what you're saying, because they're programmed to accept any explanation as valid if it follows the word "because". State what you want before "because", throw in any reason you want after it (even if the reason is bogus), and the request is seen as legitimate. "Can I hurry and cut in front of you to order my espresso, because my car's on the fritz?"

"'One word,' said the president of one of the world's largest chemical companies pulling me aside during a training session. 'Tell me one word that will help me get more out of my people, out of my sales team.' I gave him the word *because* and explained how to use it and why it works. Got a thank you card from him six weeks later: '*Because* is the most effective word I have ever used. It works like magic!'" – *Jerry Hocutt*

been there, done that. That was nothing. You should have seen the doozy I pulled.

"Wisdom comes at a price. And I have paid dearly for mine." – *Sue Grafton*

behavior, *n*. Conduct that gets you thrown off your flight: looking suspicious; mouthing "gun" to a friend you're horsing around with; staggering to your seat on the flight deck because you pulled an all-nighter in captain's lounge.

"You get more of the behavior you reward. You don't get what you hope for, ask for, wish for, or beg for. You get what you reward." – *Michel le Boeuf*

belief, *n*. What you have when you don't know. How to move forward until you do. What's missing when the sales manager asks, "Why can't you sell?"

"The branch manager asked what turned my sales around literally overnight. 'I didn't believe. I didn't believe in our product. I didn't believe in the need for our product. I didn't believe the customers I needed to find could be found. I didn't believe in our company. Once I changed my beliefs, my sales turned that very day.'" – *My reply to the CEO when he asked how I became the company's number one salesman in the nation my very first year**

believe it or not. Did you just insult me?

"Salt Lake people are reasonable, believe it or not." – *Chris Matthews*

believers, *n.pl*. Completely persuaded. Leaders. People with a purpose. What bosses want a team of. SEALs, Special Forces, Rangers.

"Rangers lead the way." – *Army Ranger motto*
"The only easy day was yesterday." – *Navy SEAL motto*

bells and whistles, *n.pl*. Twenty different wash cycles on your new washer. Distractions to what the customer really wants: a solution to her problems (clean clothes, fast and easy).

benefits, *n.pl*. Perks to keep employees happy and from going elsewhere. None required during a recession. None required for your kids because they're not going anywhere anyway.

best, *n*. Not perfect; can still stand some improvement.
"The best players don't always win. Those who play the best do." – *Pete Carroll*

best guess, *n*. A better guess than a good guess, but still, at best, only a guess.
"I saw a woman wearing a sweatshirt with 'GUESS' on it. I said 'thyroid problem?'" – *Unknown*

best in class. Try to get placed in a class with low standards and weak competitors.
"Sit by the homely girl – you'll look better by comparison." – *Debra Maffers, Miss America 1982*

Beta test, *n*. An experiment with volunteers to iron out the kinks in the prototype. First marriages.

better, *adj*. Not quite there yet, but close.
"I think men who have a pierced ear are better prepared for marriage. They've experienced pain and bought jewelry." – *Rita Rudner*

big picture, *n*. It's the future as your boss sees it; be in it.
"His family album indicates that his ancestors went west in a covered wagon. And when I saw the pictures of them, I realized why the wagon was covered." – *Unknown*

bill of goods. It's that worthless education you paid thousands for to learn the secrets for how to become a real estate mogul; the same information you could have gotten free from the Internet.

billing, *n*. Invoices with deviously designed codes and charges that even the billing department can't decipher. Hospital, telephone, and cable bills are the gold standards revered by companies wishing to hustle their customers in the same manner. But hospitals have the added advantage of giving their patients heart attacks and strokes when seeing their bills, thus resulting in readmissions and additional billings.

billing department, *n*. Where sales managers spend half their day explaining why the salespeople gave the concessions they did to close the deals – so the people in billing can keep their jobs.

"I disconnected all of the hospital's and doctors' pagers Friday night because they were sixty days in arrears in paying their bill. I knew that would force them to pay it by Monday." – *Billing department head explaining to company president her decision endangering hundreds of lives**

Bing, *n*. The search engine's Pepsi to Google's Coke.

bitchin', *adj*. Cool. "That was one bitchin' presentation!" Verbal applause.

bitcoin, *n*. Digital Monopoly money.

"A bitcoin is an analog version of the wooden nickel." – *Scott Stantis, Chicago Tribune editorial cartoonist*

blackmail, *n*. When two people know the same secret, and one of them will pay to keep it that way.

"Knowing the boss's girlfriend is called job security." – *Unknown*

blah-blah-blah, *n*. What men hear when women talk.

"Why do you have that blank stare on your face when I'm talking to you? You look like a deer caught in the headlights." – *Woman to spaced out man who only heard "blah-blah-blah"*

blitz, *n*. Saturation cold calls of office parks and buildings by a sales team. Blitz's bomb because the salespeople are hiding out in the bunkers at Starbucks, no sales are made, and they get one marginal lead that is never followed-up. Plus, the survivors tell and re-tell gruesome stories of getting thrown out onto the streets and horrify their own staff. It's like a Stephen King novel that won't end.

blog, *n*. A slog of words interesting only to the writer. Led to the birth of Twitter because bloggers use way too many characters.

blowback, *n*. It's what happened when you told the prospect at the end of your presentation, "Tell me what you honestly think. You won't hurt my feelings." Ouch! Wasn't expecting that. That hurt.

blowing smoke, *v.t.* The customer's negotiating tactic of exaggerating the competitors' proposals in hopes of getting a sweetheart deal. Big uptick in smoke blowing in some states where pot is now legal.

"The other agent said we could get the same square footage in office space on the same street a mile away – for thirty-five percent less. And the first six months are rent free!" – *Business owner*

blown away, *v.t.* When your customer is gasping in wide-eyed awe and excitement at your amazing presentation. Also, terrorists at the receiving end of a drone strike. Same thing.

bluebird, *adj*. A sale made without much effort; a gimme. When the receptionist calls over the intercom, "Sales call on line one," and the salespeople rush to be the first to pick-up, that's a bluebird calling.

Bluetooth, *n*. When someone is standing next to you waiting for the "Walk" light at the corner to change and asks a question, and turning to answer (wondering if you know her), you realize too late she's on her wireless headset. She looks at you like you're an idiot. You know the feeling.

body language, *n.* The silent language that can't hide a lie. For example, when the prospect tells the salesman he's still in the running to get the business while unknowingly shaking her head, crossing her arms, and avoiding eye contact.

"I have always thought the actions of men the best interpreters of their thoughts." – *John Locke*

boggles my mind. Amazement of a stupid act that you didn't think anyone was capable of pulling off. "How you got your head stuck way up in that part of your anatomy, I've got no idea."

boob, *n.* A stupid, awkward person caught in a booby trap who can't even spell boob backwards. It's a panel of old, male politicians holding hearings on women's reproductive rights without calling any women witnesses.

"I was so handsome that women became spellbound when I came into view. In San Francisco, in rainy seasons, I was often mistaken for a cloudless day." – *Mark Twain*

book, *n.* A shortcut to learning that can save you time, money, pain, and embarrassment. You can't live long enough to make all the mistakes yourself.

"One question I ask on interviews for a sales position is, 'What three books have you read in the past year and what did you learn from them?' Eighty percent of applicants haven't even read three books. In less than five minutes I rule them out and show them the door. Interview over. I won't hire people who aren't curious." – *Washington small business owner**

bookkeeping, *n.* A record of a company's profits and losses. Evidence of comptroller Peter robbing bookkeeper Paul to pad the annual report, and then returning to Paul what's his in time for the state's audit.

Words That Escaped Me Before My Brain Finished Downloading

bookstore, *n*. Quickly becoming a disappearing Dinostore. Where you go to preview books before ordering online.

boss, *n*. Bosses set priorities: "Do it now!" They understand when things go wrong: "What the hell happened?*!" Bosses are compassionate: "I don't give a damn!" (Notice how bosses always speak in exclamation points?!!)

brain dead, *n*. The second organ pronounced dead after the numb butt from sitting in an all-day budget meeting.

brainstorming, *n*. A group of people putting their heads together to find the solution to a problem or to create a new idea. Exciting the first time the group meets, until they find out only one person has any ideas. Rarely is a second meeting called.

"This gathering is what I call 'intimate', which really means 'Where is everybody?'" – *Tim Conway*

branch, *n*. A smaller office, usually in another town or state, that reports to headquarters. Branches in remote areas have many similarities to Russian gulags and are used as a threat veiled as a reward. "Keep missing your numbers and we're going to promote you to Nome."

branding, *n*. The best branding is done by making the name of your product synonymous with every product in your field. For example, when you say, "Let's get a Coke," you may end up getting a Pepsi or even a bottled water. When you're looking for coffee at the hotel you ask, "Is there a Starbucks nearby?" When you're at your kid's soccer tournament you ask the other parents, "Did anyone see a McDonald's on the way?"

breaking news, *n*. Hardly ever. The news station's desperate marketing ploy to stop you from changing channels. Usually only a local fire, freeway stoppage, or gas station robbery. News flash! Give me a break.

"If TV stations have real breaking news, why do they wait until the regularly scheduled news hour to deliver it?" – *Jerry Hocutt*

bribe, *n*. Under-the-table hand off for landing government contracts at national, state, and local levels. Results in jail time if caught; highly courted lobbyist if not. Political corridors are where bribes are solicited and paid with secret handshakes and greased palms.

bring it on. A cocky challenge to fate who might bring what you weren't expecting. Said by some who don't have to back it up, and get others to fight their battles for them. "My dad can beat up your dad!"

"President Bush said that American troops under fire in Iraq aren't about to pull out, and he challenged those tempted to attack U.S. forces, 'Bring them on.'" – *USA Today, July 2003*

broker, *n*. Someone who is less better off financially than you but better off than the brokest.

bucket list, *n*. Today's pick-up list for the driver for Honey Buckets.

"My favorite blanket, toys and games, candy and food, vomit bag." – *First grader when asked by teacher for their Thanksgiving project what she would have had on her list to bring over on the Mayflower**

budget cuts, *n.pl*. Early retirements for those who didn't know they'd put in for retirement. Thanks for your service.

Words That Escaped Me Before My Brain Finished Downloading

bull, *n.* Male's proper response to female companion in the passenger seat who says, "You don't have a clue where we are, do you?"

"Women can do anything men can do but are smart enough not to." – *Cal FitzSimmons*

bulleted points, *n.pl.* Language of executives. Stick to three whether you're talking, sending an email, or leaving a voicemail. Speak in nouns and verbs only.

"If it looks like a quick read, rather than a major investment of time and attention, you're likely to give it a look." – *Paul Brown*

bully, *v.* How some people try to negotiate when right is not on their side, while hoping they won't be called out.

"My dad always used to tell me that if someone challenges you to an after-school fight, tell them you won't wait – you can kick their ass right now." – *Cameron Diaz*

bumped, *v.* The airline's back-up plan to overbooking. Soon they'll realize that not only can they bump you, but they can charge you an outrageous re-booking fee for changing flights because you got bumped.

"We always overbook our flights because we don't expect everyone to show up. You'll just have to deal with it." – *Minneapolis gate agent to bumped passenger with confirmed seating**

bumper sticker, *n.* The idea behind Twitter.

"If you can read this, I've lost my trailer." – *Unknown*

bureaucracy, *n.* The destroyer of initiative contributing to cubicle mazes of unaccountability.

"I agree the instructions are ambiguous and unclear, but our hands are tied." – *IRS auditor**

burn bridges, *v.* It's either total commitment and confidence – or sheer stupidity.

The Wickedly Fun Dictionary of Business

business, *n*. What you want to have until you do.

"'How do you get started in this business?' people ask me. 'You go out and you fail,' I tell them." – *Stephen Colbert*

business casual, *n*. A fine line between dressing relaxed and looking like you're on your way to sit in a duck blind at 4 a.m.

"Showing up to work in stained, wrinkled clothing shows a lack of judgment. The perception is that lack of judgment would translate to work decisions." – *Jackie Haggerty, HR director*

business convention, *n*. A meeting place where people go to discuss ideas to grow their businesses and improve their work. At least that's the story they tell and they're sticking with it.

"Business conventions are important because they demonstrate how many people a company can operate without." – *Unknown*

business expert, *n*. Anyone who lives more than 50 miles from your location. Bosses tell their employees how to succeed and no one listens. The expert tells them the same thing and she's an oracle. No one in the expert's city will hire her because she doesn't live 50 miles distance.

"A person who reads three books on the same subject has more knowledge on that subject than 95% of other people." – *David Peoples*

business lunch, *n*. Tax write-off depending upon how the IRS examiner is feeling the day of your audit. After being seated, be sure and speak one sentence concerning business matters for complete write-off and before ordering a bottle of France's Henri Jayer Richebourg Grand Cru de Nuits for $14,395. If you can pronounce the wine's name on the first try, lunch is on the house.

business plan, *n*. The blueprint for how to build a business. Like dealing with any contractor, there will be extensive changes and remodels without any hope of the work ever being completed.

"At the time of Sarah Winchester's death (heiress to the rifle fortune), her uncompleted house went from an eight room house, to 160 rooms, with 2000 doors, 10,000 windows, 47 stairways, 47 fireplaces, 13 bathrooms, and 6 kitchens. Construction started in the late 1800's and continued until her death in 1922 and was never finished." – *The Winchester Mystery Mansion**

business-to-business handshake, *n*. Where the bottom edges of each person's right hands are parallel to the ground, and the grips meet web-to-web at the thumbs with a firm – not bone crushing – grasp. Three pumps up and down should do it. Five or more means you're lonely and looking for companionship. Not letting go will get you arrested.

"It's hard to shake hands and be hostile." – *Sandra Day O'Connor explaining why the Supreme Court Justices have the ritual of shaking hands before going into court*

but, *conj*. A word that negates everything said before it. "You're just the type of employee we're looking to hire, but we've decided to go with someone else."

butt-dial, *v*. Smart ass.

butter up, *v.i.* Greasing the ego to ease the knife in undetected.

button man, *n*. In politics, the guy who makes candidate buttons worn by conventioneers. In the underworld, the guy who closes the deal and completes the contract. In retail, your tailor.

buyers, *n.pl*. Like those in the witness protection program, they're the hardest people in the world for salespeople to find even though they're walking around in plain sight.

"Mary: 'How many times a week do people tell you you suck?' Arlo: 'Are you going to let her speak to me like this?' Stan: 'It seems like a valid question.'" – *In Plain Sight*

buying in, *v.i.* A subtle signal salespeople look for in the eyes of customers during the presentation. "Is she buying this?"

buying signal, *n.* A customer's "tell" that she likes what she sees. Such tells could include: "Wow! Will you look at that!"; a big smile; reaching for the wallet; nodding vigorously up and down; writing out a purchase order. As a rule, you'll never see such obvious tells, but you can always hope.

buyout, *n.* You're done here. Start looking for another job.

buzz marketing, *n.* Viral word-of-mouth. If it works, no sales, marketing, and advertising costs incurred. A comptroller's dream.

by the book. No creative or original ideas allowed here. Just do as you're told. (Better hope there are no errors in the book.)

C

call center, *n.* Where to find the telemarketers you hang up on. Shrewdly placed in remote areas where jobs are scarce and people would rather not work on their parents' farms.

call reluctance, *n.* Fear of cold calling. Fear of calling client to tell her that her investment has been lost. Fear to call to follow-up on the job interview.

"I couldn't do it. I was parked in front of the office park and I couldn't get out of my car and make the cold calls. I sat there for two hours. I couldn't move. I was hyperventilating, sweating, shaking – I was a nervous wreck." – *New salesman explaining why he was quitting sales on his very first day in the field**

caller i.d., *n.* A visible, electronic trap for cold callers that scammers are conniving to escape.

"Is this a cold call? How did you get my number? I'm busy. Why don't you give me your home phone number and I'll give you a call when it's inconvenient for you?" – *Jerry Seinfeld*

can I help. What better way to start a conversation with someone new?

can or could, *v*. Women, don't use *can* or *could* if you want a man to do something. Men take words literally, whereas women don't. Men see these two words as a challenge and not a call to action. "Can you do this proposal for me?" she asks. "I could," he replies, "but I'm not." (Cf. *will or would*.)

candidly, *adv*. An attempt to appear honest and forthright while trying to keep a straight face. "Candidly, I didn't do anything wrong" means "Well, it didn't seem wrong to me anyway."

canvass, *v*. In police work, to search from door-to-door looking for the crime's suspect. In sales, searching door-to-door looking for customer suspects. In both cases you could get shot.
    "Solicitors Will Be Shot – Survivors Will Be Shot Again!" – *Sign posted on door of a business in a rough and tumble industrial area**

captive audience, *n*. Passengers on a plane.
    "We'd like to invite everyone on today's flight to join our airline's credit card program and we'll include 5000 frequent flyer miles when you join. An attendant will be down the aisle in just a few minutes with the applications." – *Flight attendant**

car allowance, *n*. What you get in lieu of a company car to "cover your travel expenses." Not even close.
    "When you drive, keep in mind the cost of replacing your car." – *Unknown*

car rental, *n*. Located in dark, seedy locations near airports where you return your car full of gas (or else!) in the dead of night by dropping your keys into a lockbox, with a quick prayer that the car won't be stolen. Your next prayer is that the airport shuttle comes before you get mugged waiting for it.

carpe diem, *n*. Seize the day. The positive attitude you start off with each morning before carpe reality.

carpool lane, *n*. Topping the hill, you see the cop's red and blue lights flashing as she's pulled over the single car driver in the HOV lane who speeded past you earlier, thumbing his nose at your rush hour crawl. Your Monday morning is starting off better than expected.

cash, *n*. Thanks to the CIA dropping off oodles and oodles of it to corrupt foreign dictators in non-descript plastic bags, your tax dollars at work.

cash cow, *n*. Highly profitable business that's milked for money for other investments. Boeing. GE. Parents (mistaken as ATM's by their college kids).
   "She was bitten on the udder by an adder." – *Song by comedian Spike Jones*

cash flow, *n*. Movement of money in and out of a company that helps to determine its value. Drug cartels call it money laundering. The government calls it taxes. No difference.

cashed out, *n*. Non-cash assets converted to cash. The cash is then taken on a secretive trip on a private jet by an executive, where it is given a new home on a warm Caribbean island with no reciprocal extradition treaty.

casual Friday, *n*. Seattle.

catalyst, *n*. Mentos in the diet Coke. The signed contract to get the ball rolling. The job offer.

caveat emptor, *n*. Buyer beware; the buyer takes the risk. Printed inside the wingsuit flyer's jumpsuit.

caveat lector, *n*. Let the reader beware. What the wingsuit flyer failed to read about *caveat emptor*.

caveat venditor, *n*. Let the seller beware that if he doesn't expressly exclude liability and responsibility, he will be sued successfully. Which is why wingsuit manufacturers are one step ahead with *caveat emptor*.

Cayman Islands, *n*. Major international financial center where banks, hedge funds, and conglomerates taunt the government with their tax-free, sheltered, and stolen money to "Come and get it if you think you can!" It's where you can visit (but not bring back) your pension and trust funds that were hijacked from you by the pirates during your company's takeover. Of course, you really won't have enough money to visit the islands since your money has gone on without you already.

CEO, *n*. Chief Executive Officer. The Boss. The Big Kahuna. Where the buck stops. Where tough decisions are made that you're not going to like. The last person to the meeting.

"You report to no one, you are the CEO (duh). You are passionate about doing chief executive officer type stuff like making decisions, having a vision and being the head boss person." – *Lululemon Athletica company's job posting for a new CEO*

certainty, *n*. For business owners, threats of legal action. For salespeople, failure and rejection. For negotiators, compromise. For travelers, delayed flights and missed connections. For job seekers, discouragement from no callbacks.

CFO, *n*. Chief Financial Officer. Keeper of the purse strings. Knows where the money is buried. A money person, not a people person.

challenge, *n.* Even when a problem is called a challenge, it's still a problem.

"Illegal aliens have always been a problem in the United States. Ask any Indian." – *Robert Orben*

chamber of commerce, *n.* A tight-knit group of local businesspeople who are shy in meeting strangers at meetings designed to meet strangers. Best introduction chamber members can make to each other: "Tell me the types of customers you're looking for and I'll see if I can get you some referrals."

chance, *n.* A risk; opportunity; lucky guess. Betting $10 on 75:1 long shot "My View from the Rear" in the fourth.

"Our language is funny – a fat chance and a slim chance mean the same thing." – *Unknown*

change, *v.* Evolution; to find a new way; to find another way; to find a better way. Most happens without your consent whether you're ready or not.

"I have no problem with change. I just don't want to be there when it happens." – *Monk*

channel, *n.* How companies sell their products, whether directly through their own sales force channel, or through distributors, direct sellers, or wholesalers. If that doesn't work, spiritualists can channel.

chaos, *n.* Crazy, unorganized, exciting confusion. Mardi Gras without the parades, partying, and beads. It's Times Square any night of the week. It's getting three job offers you weren't expecting and having to make a decision by tomorrow.

"Some people never go crazy. What truly horrible lives they must lead." – *Charles Bukowski*

character flaw, *n.* Strangely, omitted from résumés.

charity, *n.* If you're giving to get a tax deduction, it's not. Charity is your daughter giving her milk and half of her sandwich to her friend at lunch who has nothing to eat.

"You give 100 percent in the first half of the game, and if that isn't enough, in the second half you give what's left." – *Yogi Berra*

cheap, *n.* It's that infomercial product you bought thinking you were getting the better part of the deal this time. On the bright side, you've got your white elephant gift for the holiday party this year.

"You are what you eat. Which makes me cheap, quick, and easy." – *Dave Thomas, founder of Wendy's*

cheap shot, *n.* Critical statement that takes unfair advantage of a known weakness. "I know the concept is hard to grasp with your tiny little pea brains. Would you like me to draw a picture with crayons?" (Second grader talking to parents.)

cheapskate, *n.* The person who invites you to lunch and then waits for you to pull out your credit card to pay for it.

check it out, *v.t.* Pretty good picture of me, don't you think?

"You know you're in trouble when the new policy on sexual harassment includes a picture of you." – *Unknown*

cheese technique, *n.* A baited trap used by the salesperson to get to first base with a prospect who refuses to consider changing vendors.

"We send a copy of the book *Who Moved My Cheese* to the buyer with this note: 'This only takes one hour to read. It talks about the importance of change. I'll call next week to see what you think.'" – *Dallas saleswoman**

cherry-picking, *v.i.* Picking the low hanging fruit. It's when the salesperson learns the competitor has gone out of business and calls on all of their orphaned customers. It even works when the customer's salesperson leaves the competitor, because the customer only has a relationship with the salesperson and has no loyalty to the company.

"I get the names of all my competitors' customers by cold calling, identifying who they're doing business with, who their salesperson is, and then keeping records on them. It's like stealing their customer lists – legally! When change is in the air, I'm the first person on the phone before my competitors know what happened. I've even had my competitors try to buy my lists when I've left that industry." – *Jerry Hocutt*

choice, *n.* Either, or. What you're stuck with. At best, several. At worse, the only.

"You have three choices in life: be good, get good, or give up." – *House, M.D.*

choose, *v.* Pick one. Requires a decision. The more choices one is given, the harder the decision; for example, paint samples. The fewer the choices, the easier the decision: heads or tails? Sometimes you're stuck with your choice (marriage) and sometimes you're not (marriage).

"Fear is a choice." – *Lee Child*

clean and simple. Keep your judgments and opinions to yourself. Just tell me what happened.

"Genius is the ability to reduce the complicated to the simple." – *C.W. Ceram*

clerk, *n.* If standing in the checkout line, find the one not talking to the customers about the weather and how their day is going and you've found the quickest line. The surlier the faster.

C-level executive, *n*. Executives on the top floors (why they need golden parachutes) in offices with a view, and with private gatekeepers. "C" is for chief: CEO, COO, CFO, CIO, CSO, CLO. Who your boss's boss reports to.

"The person who knows 'how' will always have a job. The person who knows 'why' will always be his boss." – *Diane Ravitch*

client, *n*. Too often taken for granted, neglected, and abused. Like a parent.

client files, *n.pl*. What just walked out the door on a flash drive with the fired employee.

clone, *n*. The goal of manufacturing is to make every product identical. Product recalls show they're getting close.

close, *v*. Ask for the order. What management begs their salespeople to do, but what they are afraid to do. Customers enjoy closing situations more than salespeople, as they will challenge the salesperson to ask for the order to see if he has the courage of his convictions. Most don't.

"The reason I hired you over the other two candidates is because you're the only one to ask for the job." – *Small business owner telling me why I got hired for my first sales job**

closed emotions, *n.pl*. Unemotional; stoic; poker face. A character trait that can help determine the personality of the person you're dealing with. Analytical and Driver personalities (50% of people) are among the top-level decision makers in larger companies and fall into this category. They're turned off by those who are flashy and over-the-top enthusiastic (open emotions).

closed-ended, *adj.* Questions with "yes" answers used to trick the customer into finally saying "Yes, I'll buy!" thinking they have no other choice. Smart customers see this coming from a mile away. Right?

coach, *n.* A mentor. Someone who can show you what to do, how to do it, and then make you want to do it.

"Let's get emotional! Let's get physical! Let's make them not want to play!!!" – *Coach Bob Hurley, St. Anthony's High School, three national championships, twenty-three state championships*

coach class, *n.* To get there requires going through the "walk of shame" where first class and business class passengers avert their eyes because they're embarrassed for you.

coerce, *v.t.* Using threats to influence, persuade, and convince. Customer to salesperson during a negotiation: "You've got to do better than that, or I'm taking my business elsewhere." A promise by a parent: "Do that again and you're getting a time-out missy!"

cold call, *n.* What makes cowards of us all. Cold calling is intelligence gathering. The most hated sales activity that leads to the failure of legions of salespeople. Calling them "warm" calls won't fool the salespeople because it still scares the beejezus out of them. Management should use these two words in the job description for hiring new salespeople. It will save hundreds of wasted interview hours talking with pretend salespeople who are looking for "house accounts" to babysit.

"I'm not completing the interview. I'm no longer interested in the job. Tell your sales manager that if this is what you have to do to sell, I want no part of it." – *Recent college grad revealing to salesman who took her out cold calling as part of the interview process why sales wasn't for her**

The Wickedly Fun Dictionary of Business

colleagues, *n.pl.* In-house competitors and critics.

comfort zone, *n.* An area where there is no immediate threat. Doesn't exist for a closer in baseball or for a salesperson.
 "You're not in the Army to feel comfortable." – *Lee Child*

commission only, *adj.* Requirement in a job description where the company wants the salesperson to take most of the risks while the company takes little. But it's the only way top salespeople will work, because they have the confidence in their skills and abilities. By working straight commission they can demand a higher percentage and maintain their independence. They're like the franchise quarterback in free agency.

commitment, *n.* Belief gives you hope. Commitment compels you to find a way. It's burning your ships on the enemy's foreign shore with no escape, leaving only one of two possible outcomes.

committed, *v.* Gone too far to back out now. It's sitting in the dentist's chair as she preps for your root canal, face tickling numb, and re-thinking if this was such a good idea after all.
 "I'm just going to do it because it's the right thing to do." – *Jerry Hocutt*

communication styles, *n.pl.* How people talk with each other depending upon the *stress du jour*.
 "The greatest problem in communication is the illusion that it has been accomplished." – *Daniel W. Davenport*

communications, *n.pl.* What's ironically missing at communications companies. What teens don't want with parents. What parents don't want with their parents. The circle is complete.
 "As a man grows wiser, he talks less and says more." – *Unknown*

commute, *v*. Hell on wheels.

company, *n*. A business that inflicts more harm upon itself than its competitors could hope for.
 "Companies aren't families. They're battlefields in civil war." – *Charles Duhigg*

company car, *n*. The boss's old beater given to the service department because she couldn't get a trade-in for it, and charities refused to take it.
 "Sing a country song in reverse, and you will quickly recover your car, house, and wife." – *Warren Buffett*

competitive, *adj*. A contest of skill, want, and aggression between people wanting the same prize. Fairness dictates it goes to the last person standing; but fairness doesn't always prevail.
 "Coach Pete Carroll declares all positions open to competition. Seahawks flooded with unemployed coaches' applications." – *Ray Wilson*

competitive advantage, *n*. Knowing the competitor's secrets, while being able to keep yours.
 "We steal secrets." – *Michael Hayden, former NSA and CIA director*

competitive price, *n*. The price of last resort.

competitive product, *n*. Fraternal twins.

competitor, *n*. The motivation for self-improvement and getting you out of your comfort zone to take necessary risks to grow.
 "A competitor is a guy who goes into a revolving door behind you and comes out ahead of you." – *Unknown*

complex sale, *n.* A long sales cycle affected by multiple decision makers, presentations, objections, trial closes, and surprise last minute complications. Like a teen asking if he can stay out all night on New Year's Eve.

composure, *n.* Attempting to juggle when forced to juggle when you don't know how to juggle.
 "Watching her is like watching a moose on roller skates: never particularly graceful, but certainly riveting to watch." – *Senator John McCain's presidential advisor Mark McKinnon describing Sarah Palin*

compromise, *n.* Negotiation's editing tool. Both sides decide on what they really need, and then what they'll give up to get it. Expected give-and-take in business. Will get you primaried in politics.
 "Want to learn how to negotiate better? What to do and not do? Watch TV's *Pawn Stars*." – *Jerry Hocutt*

computers, *n.pl.* Unlike people, they exist to be manipulated.
 "Men think computers should be referred to as females because: (1) No one but the creator understands their internal logic, and (2) the message 'Bad command or file name' is about as informative as 'If you don't know why I'm mad at you, I'm certainly not going to tell you.'
 "Women think computers should be referred to as males because: (1) They have a lot of data but they are still clueless, and (2) they are supposed to help you solve problems, but half of the time they are the problem." – *Unknown*

concentration, *n.* The intense focus of the bull eying the matador's dancing red cape without seeing what he's hiding behind it.
 "What's it mean to be focused? Look at the intensity of boxers just before the first bell rings." – *Unknown*

concept, *n.* An idea sometimes hard to grasp: women and shoes. Sometimes the concept is easy to grasp: men and beer.

concerns, *n.pl.* Get enough and you have a deal killer.

concession, *n.* If you give a small concession, you can ask for a greater concession in return, and the other person will be none the wiser. It's when the flight attendant asks if you'd like to have the exit row seating for more leg room comfort, and then telling you (once you're strapped in), "If there is an emergency, you're responsible for opening the emergency door and helping everyone out before you exit."

concierge, *n.* Fancy French name for hotel gal or guy Friday who makes restaurant arrangements, schedules limousine services, recommends night life hot spots, and procures show and tour tickets. How to find the city's best restaurants only the locals know about? Ask her where she takes her family for special occasions.

concise, *adj.* Brief.
    "Say it concisely and precisely." – *Captain "Sully" Sullenberger*

conclusion, *n.* Where to begin.
    "A conclusion is the place where you got tired of thinking." – *Martin H. Fischer*

conference room, *n.* An office's formal meeting room where employee, sales, and vendor meetings are held. Closed doors are to keep the uninvited out, while not letting those in, out. It's like solitary confinement with friends.

conference table, *n.* A long table in the conference room where visitors don't know where to sit. Hint: don't sit at the end where the chair faces the room's door; this is reserved for the Head Honcho.

And don't sit at the opposite end; this is reserved for the Head Honcho-in-Waiting who's eyeing the boss's chair. They both want an unobstructed, direct line-of-sight view to avoid any untoward moves by the other.

"Where to sit? Ask the customer which chair is her's, then take the seat closest to it." – *Jerry Hocutt*

confidence, *n*. Watch this!

"Confidence is what you have before you understand the problem." – *Woody Allen*

confident, *adj*. Pretty sure.

"Even if you're not the best, you've got to be confident that you're better than the other guy." – *Ron Darling*

confidential, *adj*. Information and admissions you don't want leaving the confessional. The problem is that too many people mistake the bar at happy hour as a confessional.

confidentiality agreement, *n*. Secret talks where all parties agree not to tell the others' secrets, unless springing a leak or two will be to their advantage.

"Sometimes you get the best answers in silence while people talk to fill the void." – *Bob Woodward*

confuse, *v.t*. What you do to others when you don't know what you're talking about. "What was I saying? I forgot what I was talking about."

confused, *adj*. The look on the other person's face when she realizes you don't know what you're talking about.

confusion, *n*. A mess you can't get out of because you didn't know what you were talking about. "Crap!"

Words That Escaped Me Before My Brain Finished Downloading

conglomerate, *n*. A mega corporation made up of many parts. It's like the body, where the right hand doesn't know what the left hand is doing.

congratulate, *v.t*. Stifled happiness for someone who got what you deserved more. "Congratulations on winning employee of the year and the free European vacation." (Loser!)

connected, *adj*. You've got "people".
 "Call my agent. Get him to post my bail." – *Pro athlete*

connecting flight, *n*. Landing late at Terminal A, you realize it leaves from Terminal D in twenty minutes. You get there as the plane is being pushed back from the gate, and in time to see all the passengers smiling and waving "bye-bye" to you from out of their tiny little windows.
 "Don't worry. There'll be another flight in four hours. Maybe we can get you on that." – *Chicago O'Hare gate agent**

connect-the-dots, *adj*. The person who wants you to complete the picture already knows the answer, but knows the answer will mean more to you if you discover it on your own. He's also testing your desire to see if you really want to know what you'll find.
 "Follow the money." – *Deep Throat*

consciously competent, *adj*. The second highest level of competence. It's the back-up quarterback who's still searching for his rhythm to make the plays work, who doesn't trust his instincts, and who misreads zone coverage and throws the interception. More study and practice are required, but he's capable of taking over in emergency situations. (See *consciously incompetent, unconsciously competent, unconsciously incompetent*.)

consciously incompetent, *adj*. The second lowest level of competence. You're stupid and you know it. Why the *Dummies* and *Idiots* books are so popular. (See *consciously competent, unconsciously competent, unconsciously incompetent*.)

consequences, *n.pl*. What you suffer when you fail to pay attention to the details. Why ships end up on the rocks because the captain didn't read the navigational and tide charts correctly.
"If there are no consequences for the behavior, there is no incentive to change them." – *Necessary Roughness*

consistent, *adj*. Steady; repetitive. What it takes to get the job done.
"Peter Marshall: 'If you're going to make a parachute jump, you should be at least how high?' Charlie Weaver: 'Three days of steady drinking should do it.'" – *Hollywood Squares*

consult, *v*. Asking the doctor, "What do you think?" If told to lose weight and exercise, another's consult is needed.
"To accept good advice is but to increase one's own ability."
– *Johann Wolfgang von Goethe*

consultant, *n*. An outside change agent. Not well received by those clinging to the status quo.
"I'm not asking for easy. I'm asking for possible." – *Brad Meltzer*

consultative selling, *n*. A salesperson selling you what he wants to sell you, while pretending to sell you what you say you want. A prerequisite to becoming a magician.

consumer, *n*. The customer, the client, the buyer, the stiff, the stooge, the sucker, the mark; depends upon how he feels after the purchase.

contact, *v.* Those who initiate contact – be it for a job or a sale – have the courage and conviction sought by those who can give them what they want.

"I may not find you – but I will never stop looking." – *The Firm*

contact us, *v.i.* Link on a company's website for how to reach them via email. Doesn't mean they'll reach back or even care. Think of it as a digital voicemail.

contract, *n.* Putting in writing what neither party trusts the other says he'll do. Only as good as your lawyer. If you're a mob boss, a hit.

contractor, *n.* Someone you hire to remodel, repair, or improve your home or office on his schedule.

control freak, *n.* Someone who won't let go. "Trust no one" is their mantra. Mistaken for dictators (who have actual guns and armies) who also won't give up control. If you notice any radical changes in your balance sheet from last year, see who's counting the money.

controller, *n.* Comptroller; chief accounting officer for a business. Doesn't like paying salespeople commissions and wants to keep the money for the company because, as she sees it, "anyone can sell – but not everyone can keep their money." She's probably right on the second part.

"Most of her sales come from add-on business. Let's turn those accounts into house accounts and let customer service take care of them and avoid any commissions." – *Controller for a Fortune 1000 company to the executive vice president**

COO, *n.* Chief Operating Officer. The CEO's right-hand man. The COO is to the CEO what a wife is to a husband: they're in charge, they know things, they get things done, and they can separate warring factions by using common sense.

cooked books, *n.pl.* Whether they're baked, broiled, poached, or fried the shareholders don't like the smell of it.

cooling off period, *n.* Grace period given to buyers to renege on their purchase when they come to their senses. Like getting an annulment after a wild night in Sin City.

corporate, *n.* The company's Vatican. Where all the C-level executives meet in secret enclaves to establish policies, procedures, and strategies. The white smoke doesn't mean they've picked a new leader. It only means one of them didn't know how to use the microwave for the popcorn.

cost cutting, *n.* It's like wranglers thinning out the herd on the cattle drive: keep what will bring top dollar and leave the weak and stragglers behind for the wolves. Culled out in this order: expenses, goods from vendors, employees, benefits, bonuses, management. Head 'em up, move 'em out!

"Sometimes you have to lay off employees to save the business. It's like being the captain in the lifeboat. You have to throw some of the people overboard in hopes you can save the boat and come back and rescue them later." – *Small business owner**

cost-benefit analysis, *n.* How customers decide whether it's worth doing business with you. How employers decide whether to keep you. How parents decide whether to have kids.

"Imagine we did not own it. How much would we think it's worth?" – *Daniel Kahneman*

count, *v.* To add, subtract, multiply, and divide. Necessary when taking inventory and counting profits. When the count is off, it's never in your favor.

"There are three kinds of people: the ones who can count – and the ones who can't." – *Unknown*

covert, *adj.* Hidden from sight. All the hidden taxes, surcharges, change fees, airport fees, and baggage fees on your airline ticket that won't come to light until you reserve your seat. Airline executives humorously refer to passengers as hostages who pay their own ransoms.

CPA, *n.* Certified Public Accountant. The best are ex-IRS agents who know how close to the edge of the precipice they can go in classifying expenses and deductions. But don't call to shoot the breeze, because they bill in six minute increments.

"An accountant uses his personality for birth control." – *Unknown*

crapshoot, *n.* Direct mail. Cover your bets and roll the dice.

"Three of the most important things I've learned from sending millions of direct mail pieces? One: have a product the recipients want. Two: pay very close attention to the names you buy from your list broker. Three: if possible, write it yourself, because no one knows your product better than you." – *Jerry Hocutt*

crazy, *n.* Definitely an asset for doing business.

"It helps if the hitter thinks you're a little crazy." – *Nolan Ryan*

creative, *adj.* What the IRS is looking for when auditing your books.

"Why does a slight tax increase cost you $200 and a substantial tax cut save you 38¢?" – *Peg Bracken*

credibility, *n*. When someone says "Trust me", they've lost it.

credit check, *n*. When salespeople hold their breath after landing a new account in hopes of getting approval. The billing department's favorite part of the selling process because they can make the salespeople grovel or cry like babies over a minor discrepancy, like the client's bankruptcy a year ago.

crisis, *n*. If they're manufactured, you're in Congress. If they're real, you're in business. They not only expose problems but set their own deadlines for solving them.

criticism, *n*. Never "constructive" even if intended to be. What the critic is saying is, "This is the way I would do it." And what the criticized is thinking is, "Yeah, if you had the cojones."
   "A critic has been defined as someone who comes down from the mountain after the battle and shoots all the wounded." – *Sander Vanocur*

critics, *n.pl*. People who push their beliefs as the absolute truths as the real truths pass them by. The same people who said the world is flat, man can never fly, and there is no such thing as evolution. Yeah, listen to your critics. They're on top of it.
   "A critic is a gong at a railroad crossing clanging loudly and vainly as the train goes by." – *Christopher Morley*

CRM, *n*. Customer Relationship Management. Software for salespeople to keep detailed records on customers: personal information, buying habits, business quirks. Will make salespeople better and more efficient. Not used by salespeople because "it's too much work." That, and they don't want their managers to know what they're up to.

cross-sell, *v.i.* What drives sales managers mad because their salespeople don't do it. Easy sale to make since it's to an existing customer. But salespeople feel it's too pushy and unprofessional. Tough.

cubicle, *n.* A worker's private office space without the office or the privacy. No need to knock. No door.

cue, *n.* A signal that can be spoken, heard, or seen but is often missed or ignored. "Why didn't you ask for the order when he handed you the check?" the incredulous sales manager asked. "I didn't think the time was right," replied the salesman.

curiosity, *n.* No discoveries have been made without it. That, and it kills cats.

"You don't seem to understand. When I said 'no', I didn't mean 'I want to know.' I meant 'No. I don't want to know.'" – *Middle school son to dad who was giving lengthy explanation about historical event the son had no interest in**

customer, *n.* The prosecutor, judge, and jury of the salesperson's offering. Once the salesperson has made her best case, it's out of her hands and she must wait for the verdict. Appeals are sometimes possible to higher authorities or if better evidence is found.

customer centric, *n.* A company that is completely focused on the customers and tries to meet their every need. Like grandparents are to grandkids.

customer expectations, *n.pl.* What a salesperson hypes to get the customer's hopes high in order to buy. It's best to set low expectations so that when they're exceeded the customer is ecstatic. "I can't guarantee the parachute will open on every jump, but it usually does. Let me know what happens."

customer focused, *n*. A customer's belief that the customer comes first. Quickly dispelled by a trip to the DMV.

"A woman is fighting the DMV to get all her surname – Keihanaikukauakahihuliheekahaunaele – on her Hawaiian driver's license." – *Seattle Times*

customer profile, *n*. Not unlike a terrorist profile. A quick way to pick the suspects out from the crowd.

"Go through our customer files and find five to seven things they all have in common." – *Sales manager to new sales hire to show her how to develop a profile of the types of customers to look for**

customer retention, *n*. Like water retention, only better, because this is something you want to keep.

customer satisfaction, *n*. Measured by repeat orders, referrals, and testimonials.

"Satisfaction is based upon expectation." – *Unknown*

customer service, *n*. A pleasant surprise to many customers. If you have to brag you have it, you don't.

customer support, *n*. The people who have to make happen what the salesperson promised. Miracle workers.

"Hey, I'm just told to get the business. It's your job to make it happen." – *Salesman to technician who has to make two-way radio units work in underground transit tunnel**

cut to the chase, *v.i.* What executives demand from those who interrupt their activities. Speak in bulleted points. Use facts, numbers, percentages, nouns, and verbs. Leave out adjectives, adverbs, and conjunctions.

"Master 'One Minute Meetings'. When someone comes in with or without an appointment, make them uncomfortable. Stand up. They won't sit down. Your actions tell them to be brief, get to the point, and leave. By standing, you will also think 20% faster because your heart rate increases by ten beats per minute. Plus, you're more alert and will make quicker decisions." – *Jerry Hocutt*

cutting edge technology. It's outdated before you can say it.

CYA, *n*. Cover Your Ass. Genius marketing plan devised by insurance companies pushing medical malpractice policies. Aided and abetted by medical suppliers who oversell their medicines, products, and equipment to encourage doctors to perform unnecessary procedures to cover their ass. An unexpected boon for ambulance chasers now that they have deep pockets to go after.

"Anybody can sue. Winning is a different matter. But when you sue, you want to find who has the most money and deepest pockets and go after them first." – *Tort law school professor indoctrinating first-year class on the nuances of the legal profession**

D

data driven, *n*. 11010011 10001101 10101010. Someone more intimate with numbers than with people.

"My doctor told me to stop having intimate dinners for four – unless there are three other people." – *Orson Wells*

dead fish handshake, *n*. Gives the perception of being a wuss. The quickest way to be shown the door on a job interview. Something that smells and should be gutted. Those who have it are surprised when told they do. The most misunderstood handshake in America because it's interpreted as a sign of weakness. It's not. It means that person probably works with their hands for a living (doctor, dentist, nurse); has a sport or hobby where they use their hands (golf, knitting, musician); or has a physical challenge and can't give a firm handshake. Such shakers don't want someone to crush their hands and ruin their livelihood.

"If an applicant for a sales position gives me the dead fish handshake, I rule them out (snapping her fingers) just like that!" – *Sales manager for a Silicon Valley tech firm**

deadline, *n*. Outside forces that compel action – ready or not.

"The show doesn't go on because it's ready; it goes on because it's 11:30." – *Lorne Michaels, SNL*

deadlock, *n*. A standoff when negotiations break down and wait for an external event to tip the scales. It happened in the 2012 NFL season when the Seattle Seahawk's receiver caught a last second Hail Mary pass for a questionable winning touchdown against Green Bay and broke a three months' referee lockout by the league.

"Success often comes just the last day, the last hour, that you're about to give up." – *Unknown*

deal, *n*. Final negotiated agreement where you feel like you came out on the short end. Almost any compromise with your kids.

deal killer, *n*. When the job applicant – on the first interview – is asked to name her greatest strength and she replies, "I'm a great talker."

debrief, *v.t.* Spit it out. Tell us what you know. Waterboarding may be involved.

"People don't ask questions they don't want answers to." – *Royal Pains*

deceptive advertising, *n*. Dating websites.

"My last girlfriend was pretty wild in bed. She used to cover me from head to toe with oil, and then set me on fire." – *David Corrado*

deceptive packaging, *n*. Potato chips.

decision maker, *n*. The decider. Doesn't always make the best decisions, but does make the final ones. Made worse when the decider skewers the facts to support his decision.

"Decisions have to be made with imperfect and inaccurate information." – *Donald Rumsfeld*

decisions, *n.pl.* Best guesses.

"If I wasn't making mistakes, I wasn't making decisions." – *Robert W. Johnson, founder of Johnson & Johnson*

decoy, *n.* Something that looks like the real deal but isn't. Substituting a similar – not identical – product to see if the customer can be fooled. "Think she'll notice?"

"We asked for a smoke-free room and the one you gave us smells like an ash tray! All you did was spray some air freshener in it." – *Irate Cleveland hotel guest**

dedicated, *adj.* Committed – until fault is found. "We're dedicated to your branch's success. You better not screw it up."

"This is dedicated to the one I love...." – *The Shirelles, 1961*

deduce, *v.t.* The fact that none of your voicemails or emails are being returned would lead you to conclude that: (a) your message needs tweaking; (b) the decision has been made and it's not in your favor; or (c) your kids don't want to talk with you.

"Call your voicemail and leave yourself a message. Then go back and listen to it. Would you call yourself back after hearing that?" – *Houston senior vice president**

deduction, *n.* A method of evaluation made famous by Sherlock Holmes; a conclusion reached by subtracting parts from the whole. It's like Michelangelo chipping away all the chunks of marble that don't look like David.

deep discount, *n.* The market dictating the product's real worth.

default, *n.* Robotic statements and actions made without thinking. The flight attendant's preflight safety instructions, matched by the passengers' (yawn) inattention.

delusion, *n.* A belief that something is – but knowing deep down it isn't.

"This is our year!" – *Every baseball fan's belief on opening day*

demand, *v.* To ask – with a threat – to have what doesn't belong to you. "I demand respect!"

"Why do you get hurt? Not because of what people do, but because you have demanded they should do as you wish." – *Vernon Howard*

demo, *n.* Proof the product will do as you say. And then it won't.

"As the new dictation system began smoking on the customer's desk during the presentation, the salesman calmly removed his jacket, placed it over the unit, and began raising and lowering the scorching coat to see if the fire was smothered. Without missing a beat he continued his spiel, 'And if the unit doesn't always work, you can send smoke signals.'" – *Salesman demonstrating his system to an attorney**

department head, *n.* A middle manager with limited decision powers.

"Go ask your mom." – *Dad**

departments, *n.pl.* Fiefdoms within a company ruled over by their own lords who are always at war with each other for budget dollars, power, and control. Think of the extended family getting together for the holidays and you get the picture.

deposit, *n.* A scam. Money given for security to get something like office space or an apartment with the promise it will be returned if all conditions are met when moving out. They never are and it never is.

"I'd return your deposit but I can't since my wife needs an operation." – *Apartment owner to tenants moving out as his justification for keeping their deposit**

depression, *n.* Sadness caused by losing a major account after doing everything you could to save it, before understanding that everything that can be saved may not want to be saved.

desire, *v.* To want what you can't have.
"Our people want a government that's better – not one that's gone!" – *Jon Stewart*

details, *n.pl.* Small things that, if not taken care of, could be disastrous; like the missing pin on the grenade. Before leaving the fast-food drive-up window don't you always check your order? It's why athletes study game films: to see what they're doing right and wrong so they can improve their game, and to pick up any "tells" that give their opponents away so they can take advantage of them.
"You don't need to be a genius to succeed in this business. You do, however, need to take care of the details." – *Plaque on the wall of the chairman of the Zales Corp. (circa 1973)**

devil in the details, *n.* It's why you double-check your bungee cord connections. "We got the bid for the bridge replacement. It looks good, but we need a closer examination to see if it meets the specs." If it's the lowest bidder, the devil it does.
"What the hell! What island is this?" – *Air Force RC -135 pilot to navigator when landing on a Pacific island over 250 miles away from the one they should have been landing on (and their squadron's mission was international map making!)**

dialing for dollars, *v.t.* Telemarketing term used to create motivation in salespeople to keep them cold calling. It's like telling your kid that if she studies hard enough, she'll get a Rhodes Scholarship. Fat chance in both situations.

dialogue, *n*. A give and take discussion to find common ground and interests. "If you interrupt me again," warned the boss, "I'm going to can you!"

"Never miss a good chance to shut up." – *Will Rogers*

different rules. The executive rule book that you're not allowed to see or play by. It's like playing "go fish" with your grandkids who make the rules up as they go and you have to play along with them.

dignity, *n*. What you lose at your power breakfast when someone tells a joke and you laugh so hard you blow milk out your nose.

dilemma, *n*. When the manager is faced with hiring someone with years of experience or someone with a greater passion for the job.

"A politician is faced with a dilemma when trying to save both sides of his faces at once." – *John Lincoln*

direct, *adj*. If the person you're dealing with doesn't beat around the bush in asking for what he wants and telling you what he thinks, then you're dealing with a Driver personality. Probably your boss.

"I'm going to reach out with a hook if you don't shut up." – *Simon Cowell*

direct mail, *n*. Spam with a stamp.

"If you're tricked into opening a direct mail piece as thinking it's as important as the envelope says it is – and it isn't – don't you lose all trust with that company instantly?" – *Jerry Hocutt*

direct sales, *n*. Friends selling friends such things as cookware, jewelry, and cosmetics. Called home parties to avoid the illegal status of pyramid schemes.

The Wickedly Fun Dictionary of Business

disability insurance, *n.* Pays if you get kneecapped or wounded when doing your cold calls; can only collect if you live to tell about it. Otherwise, see *life insurance*.

disappointment, *n.* Getting what you expected, but not what you wanted.

"Diogenes was asked why he begged money from a statue. He replied, 'I am practicing disappointment.' He was working on his response." – *H.A. Dorfman*

disapproved, *v.* You're expense report with a winking smiley face.

discipline, *n.* Doing what must be done, and what you don't want to do, to reach your goal.

"The key is not the 'will to win'. Everybody has that. It is the will to *prepare* to win that is important." – *Bobby Knight*

disclaimer, *n.* When the waiter sets the plate in front of you warning, "It's hot!" (and you still touch it anyway).

"The chef said the bugs are in your salad because the lettuce came from our own organic garden." – *Waiter at a four-star restaurant outside Portland, Oregon, explaining to the appalled diner why she had the uninvited visitors sharing her greens**

discount, *n.* The true price, because the sticker price was inflated to make it look like a bargain.

discourage, *v.t.* To dissuade, sometimes unintentionally, and sometimes on purpose.

"So, you want to start your own business like mine? Here, let me show you the twenty-four state sales tax forms I have to complete each quarter. Then I'll show you eleven of their state income tax forms." – *Advice to entrepreneur wanting to be a national speaker**

discreet, *adj*. Not telling your boss his fly is open as he's giving his presentation, while frantically motioning up and down with your hand in hopes he'll get the message.

disinformation, *n*. Intentional fictional facts that bomb, like WMDs; propaganda. Planted false information mastered by politicians and visited upon the unsuspecting public.

"The truth is more important than the facts." – *Frank Lloyd Wright*

disputes, *n.pl*. Never pretty. Lots of name calling and finger pointing. Lots of huffing and puffing. Most settled amicably, but not satisfactorily, for all involved.

"The best fight is the one you don't have." – *Lee Child*

disqualify, *v.t*. To remove from consideration. The best way to qualify a prospect is to try and disqualify him first. The top three disqualifiers: (1) need, (2) want, and (3) money. Easily observed in certain "dating" activities near Times Square and on the Las Vegas strip.

distinctions, *n.pl*. How to identify things that look identical but aren't. For example, every fingerprint is unique and distinct. Only the experts can tell the difference. Salespeople are the fingerprint experts and must show the customers what makes them different from the competition because, "You all look alike."

"If customers can't tell you apart from the competition, they start looking at the little things. The small things. The trivial things." – *Harry Beckwith*

diversion, *n*. Social media that has a higher priority than your work.

"In case of fire, please exit building before tweeting about it." – *Sign in office*

DNA, *n*. Like kids, it doesn't lie. In a company, the DNA starts at the top and is passed on to everyone below.

"My father had a profound influence on me – he was a lunatic." – *Spike Milligan*

Do Not Call Registry, *n*. The inscription on the tombstone of telemarketing.

dog and pony show, *n*. When a salesperson trots out her products and makes them jump through the hoops like she's a lion tamer for Ringling Bros.

"Odd things, animals. All dogs look up to you. All cats look down at you. Only a pig looks at you as an equal." – *Winston Churchill*

dominance, *n*. In a position of supreme power and control where everyone must bow to your every command – a newborn.

"The only one who controls me is me, and that's just barely possible." – *John Lennon*

dork, *n*. He's the one who teamed up with the nerd and the geek and created that website they just sold for $4 billion.

double-talk, *n*. It makes sense, but you know it's nonsense. The health insurance company's justification for why their premiums are increasing by 32% again this year.

"Let's try that again...you were where last night?" – *Teen's parent**

doubt, *v*. Belief's killer. "I bet we'll get upgraded to first class." I doubt it.

down payment, *n*. The hook of commitment to ensure you follow through to complete the deal. The engagement ring.

downside, *n*. Winning the largest Powerball lotto in history and having to keep it a secret so the leeches won't find you.

"I'm giving away five Powerball lotto tickets to five lucky attendees today. I only have two requirements if you win: first, please give 10% to your favorite charity. Second, if you win, do not – I repeat – do not call me and tell me that you won!" – *Jerry Hocutt*

downsize, *v*. Legal age discrimination by doing away with your job classification and you just happen to be the only one in it.

drama, *n*. Scene inside sales manager's office where two salespeople are duking it out for selling in the same territory. Get out the yellow tape, this is fast becoming a crime scene.

drama queen, *n*. Chicken Little with social media access.

drawback, *n*. A negative hesitation to endorse a positive event. "The only drawback to sending our salespeople to the public seminar is that the other companies attending might try to recruit them." Okay, so not all drawbacks are so bad.

dress code, *n*. Standard of dress expected by businesses. How you dress affects your attitude and how others react to you. Wear an orange jumpsuit to the mall with D.O.C. stenciled on the back and see the reactions you get.

"He's still recovering from injuries he suffered when he went to a costume party dressed as a piñata." – *Unknown*

drive, *n*. Mission passion.

"When I die, I want to die like my grandfather – who died peacefully in his sleep. Not screaming like all the passengers in his car." – *Unknown*

Driver personality, *n*. Someone with a dominant, pushy, impatient attitude. One of the four major personalities (see *Expressive, Amiable, and Analytical personalities*). 15% of the people you deal with. Don't care what they say or if they hurt your feelings. Have no patience in dealing with the Amiable personalities as they're seen as weak and too touchy-feely. Motto: "It's my way or the highway!" On the plus side, they make decisions quickly and like facts, figures, and charts. Big picture people. Talk to them in bulleted points – not in complete sentences, and definitely not in paragraphs. All correspondence should fit on a Post-It note.

droning on, *v.t.* A bombing conversation you don't want to be the target of.
"Try and talk plain." – *Harvey Penick*

DST, *n*. Daylight Savings Time. It's the day after the states go off standard time and when you arrive later than you anticipated at the Oahu airport, but still thirty minutes before your flight departs to the mainland. But then you learn Hawaii isn't on DST and your flight already left without you.

due diligence, *n*. Doing your homework so you won't be caught by surprise and so you'll have the edge.
"When the press talks about my successes as a Senate majority leader they always emphasize my capacity to persuade, to wheel, and deal. Hardly anyone ever mentions that I usually had more and better information than my colleagues." – *Lyndon B. Johnson*

dumb down, *v.t.* Changes to the speech required by the company's chief engineer for her presentation to the board of directors.

dumb luck, *n*. Finally getting a decent driver's license photo.

E

early adopters, *n.pl.* Tech nerds and geeks lined up outside the Apple stores two days before the new release and paying twice the price for products still with bugs to be worked out.

ebook, *n.* The wrecking ball of brick and mortar booksellers. A cruel hoax for Evelyn Woods speed readers whose finger reading continually flips the pages at the end of each line.

"People believe what they read. They think no one would write it down if it wasn't the truth." – *Biloxi Blues*

educate, *v.* Don't tell your customer about your product, rather let her use it so she will learn about it. Experience, not words, teaches.

"I say touch can be learned. I don't say touch can be taught. The way you learn touch is by practice. There is no other way." – *Harvey Penick, legendary golf instructor*

eggshells, *n.pl.* A tightrope you walk on when telling the truth to a client you want to keep as a customer.

"People think that if they avoid the truth, it might change to something better before they have to hear it." – *Marsha Norman*

ego, *n*. The personality's cataract.

"The voice in your head is your ego." – *Criminal Minds*

elephant in the room. Refusing to see the truth, while diverting your attention to more appealing matters. It's like standing on the bathroom scales as you're eating your Klondike bar.

"They couldn't hit an elephant at this dist...." – *Supposed last words of Union General John Sedgwick before being hit by sniper fire*

elevator, *n*. A good place to have fun, practice your cold calling, and get over your agoraphobia during your lunch hour as you hold an empty cage and ask each person entering, "Did you happen to see any of my infected lab rats on your floor?"

elevator speech, *n*. Making a case why the prospect needs what you sell in thirty seconds or less. It's the job applicant's message to employers at job fairs. It's the Girl Scout's approach for cookie sales outside the local supermarket. It's a test to match your spiel with the listener's rapidly diminishing attention span.

"Two seats on the forty-yard line – $240!" – *Ticket scalper outside gates of sold out college game**

eliminate prospects, *v.t*. Don't cold call to *find* new prospects, call to *eliminate* them. By eliminating prospects you're taking the identical activities it takes to find new ones, but you're having greater success while taking the pressure off yourself. It's the same elimination process HR uses to cull résumés for new job postings.

email, *n*. For the passive-aggressives, the "Send" button should be replaced with "Really?" Just because you can say it, doesn't mean you should send it.

"Over 420 billion emails are generated by Americans daily." – *Washington Post, June 2013*

email address, *n.* The lock to your email picked by spammers.

embarrassment, *n.* The keynote speaker being told just before going on stage that she had her lavaliere microphone turned on for all to hear in the ballroom when she was in the ladies room.

emotions, *n.pl.* Feelings like anger, fear, love, excitement. The sizzle that sells the steak. People buy the big screen TV with emotions and justify with logic as they carry it to their car.

"Anger and fear are feelings. Don't let your feelings control what you do or don't do. Play with a yo-yo. It will distract your feelings long enough to change them and allow you to do what you should be doing." – *Monk*

empathy, *n.* "I understand. And because I do, I can help." Not to be confused with sympathy, which is to feel the hurt and to be too paralyzed to help.

"I know...for I have been there." – *Mark Twain*

empty suit, *n.* The Peter Principle with a spiffy tie.

empty threat, *n.* A peacock spreading its tail feathers to look larger in hopes of scaring away a real threat. A negotiator threatening to walk out if a trivial demand isn't met. Your child holding his breath until he gets his way.

encourage, *v.t.* To inspire and offer support in difficult situations. "Look," the drill sergeant bellowed, "you're either going to jump or I'm going to push you!"

"You'll remember these next 30 minutes for the rest of your life." – *The only comments made by the undefeated Wichita Falls (Texas) high school football coach who had written the words on the blackboard in the locker room at half-time in the state championship game, and their closest game of the year; his team won to remain undefeated (1961)**

end user, *n.* The person in the buyer's organization who is stuck using the product the boss bought even though the boss has no idea how it works, why he bought it, or if it will do as promised.

energy drink, *n.* Whole-body Viagra.
 "I'm 40. I don't want a drink that gives me more energy. I want a drink that gives me hope." – *Nick Griffin*

enthusiasm, *n.* If it's real, it's exciting. If it's manufactured, it's a con.
 "I rate enthusiasm even above professional skill." – *Sir Edward Appleton*

entrepreneur, *n.* Someone who starts their own business because they got fed up working for numbskulls who wouldn't listen to new ideas for how to improve their company, services, or products. They're headstrong people who are so opinionated that no one else will hire them. Entrepreneurs believe they'll always find a way.

epiphany, *n.* Aha! A sudden realization that you've found the answer. Often comes in the shower where you have nothing to write it down. Note to self: best ideas come in the shower; take more showers.

equity, *n.* An interest in something that you nurture hoping it will increase in value and become an asset. Sometimes a long shot. "I'll go with $100 on the Jets by three."
 "Americans spend $300 billion every year on games of chance, and that doesn't even include weddings and elections." – *Argus Hamilton*

escalation, *n.* To ramp up; to increase in intensity. Attorneys will include escalation clauses in a contract as a motivator. Cowboys call them spurs. Too much unnecessary escalation and the horse will buck you on your butt.

esprit de corps, *n*. All for one, and one for all. Why it doesn't exist in business? Money, greed, power, and control.

"The few. The proud. The Marines." – *Semper Fi*

established procedure, *n*. "That's the way things have always been done around here and we're not changing." Similar to an infection that's not doctored and can lead to paralysis or death.

ethics, *n.pl*. Not even a speed bump between lobbyists and politicians.

"You can't be an engineer for this company if you have no grasp of business ethics. You leave me no choice. I'm putting you on the management fast track." – *Dilbert*

event, *n*. A meeting, seminar, or trade show. Those who plan events never attend those events, otherwise they'd quit planning them. The only anticipation is "When will this thing be over?"

"We don't control events. We can only respond to events." – *Unknown*

evolved, *v.t*. Gotten older. Wiser? TBD.

"If Darwin was right, you will probably figure it out in a few million years." – *Unknown*

EVP, *n*. Executive Vice President. The top dog of all the vice presidents. Has the best tennis game.

example, *n*. What you don't want to be – good or bad.

exceed expectations, *v.t*. A ticket through the school zone.

exclusive right, *n*. What manufacturers give to certain distributors to give them an advantage by not making their products available to anyone else. A father giving his daughter in marriage.

The Wickedly Fun Dictionary of Business

excuse me, *v.t.* Sarcastic comeback to denigrate another person's accurate observation. "That was a stupid thing to say to the customer," the supervisor said. "Well, *excu-u-u-use* me!"

excuses, *n.pl.* Explanations are used for why it didn't work. Excuses are used for why you didn't try.
"Trying reveals the 'how'." – *Jerry Hocutt*

executive, *n.* C-level bigwigs who relish political games and intrigue.
"Why join the navy when you can be a pirate?" – *Steve Jobs*

executive assistant, *n.* The executive's boss.

exit interview, *n.* When companies hear the truth too late. It's the three-term Senator who decides not to run for office again and then writes a tell-all book of what a "corrupt institution" she's been a part of (although unashamedly keeping her lifetime benefits and exorbitant pension for her contributions towards the fraud).
"What causes military disasters? Being too late." – *General Douglas MacArthur*

expense, *n.* The cost of doing business. A legitimate tax write-off. Some are like candy – they're fudged.

expense report, *n.* Like some bras, padded.

experience, *n.* Giving birth and not just holding the hand and giving encouragement. What companies want, but don't want to pay for. Experience is measured by not making the same mistakes twice.
"Ask the experienced rather than the learned." – *Arabian Proverb*
"Experience has been defined as 'compulsory education'." – *Unknown*

"We learn from experience. A man never wakes up his second baby just to see it smile." – *Grace Williams*

experienced only need apply. Seen in job postings where employers are hoping to get a brain surgeon at minimum wage.

"Experience is what you get when you don't get what you want. And experience is often the most valuable thing you have to offer." – *Randy Pausch*

expert, *n*. Someone you don't want to pay for their experience because you saw a video for how to do it yourself.

"I thought it would fall the other way." – *Homeowner explaining to local news reporter why he didn't hire a logger to fell the 80-foot cedar in his front yard that he decided to topple himself – and then it crushed his house**

express warranty, *n*. A written promise you can show the judge. What you wish people came with.

Expressive personality, *n*. A person whose favorite subject is himself; always the center of attention. His favorite song: *Give Me All You Got*. His favorite book: *Me Before You*. His favorite magazine: *Me*. Expressives account for 15% of the people you meet (see *Driver, Analytical, and Amiable personalities*), make decisions quickly, but have poor follow-up. If they have photos in their office, they're turned out facing the guests and they're photos of themselves standing or sitting with politicians, sports stars, or Hollywood personalities. They can't deal with Analyticals because they demand facts, accuracy, and patience. Cars are sporty, bling is excessive, and clothes are loud. And if they can afford it, they have their own private jet with their name emblazoned on the side.

"I've given up reading books. I find it takes my mind off myself." – *Oscar Levant*

extemporaneous, *adj*. The goal of every speech, presentation, and cold call. You're so well rehearsed that you sound spontaneous. It's like rolling in home late after last call and you've rehearsed your excuse so well that it trips off the tongue without a glitch. But if your tongue gets ripped out, you had a "tell"; more rehearsals required.

extended warranty, *n*. The service department's profit center.
"For only $21 more you can get an extended three year warranty on top of the manufacturer's lifetime warranty." – *Clerk at big-box office supply store**

extortion, *n*. Fees for changing your flight schedule.

extrovert, *n*. A bubbly, enthusiastic, exciting person who never has a bad day and who bugs the hell out of you.

eyes, *n.pl*. Where the truth lies. "I can see through your lyin' eyes."

F

FABs, *n*. Features, Advantages, Benefits. A feature is the button on the product. An advantage is what the button does. A benefit is what the button provides. When selling, start with the benefit. Works on something as simple as a Powerball lotto ticket. "Win $590 million!" (Benefit.) You look over your number selections (feature), and then pick your winning six (advantage).

"Some things seem unlikely. But someone always wins the lottery." – *Stephen King*

Facebook, *n*. Are you sure there's not something more productive and meaningful you should be doing with your life? Social media site used to create envy among friends, post pictures of the foods you eat, and to be used as a weapon by HR to deny you a job. Can't be confirmed, but all your messages are read by the incarcerated in prisons trolling for online dates. Please post glamour shot.

"Early (Stone Age) social networking: 'Hey everybody, look at my rock!'" – *The Flying McCoys*

Facebook fatigue, *n*. Had all the drama I can stand. Please cancel my account.

faces, *n.pl*. What you remember without the names.

"After a certain number of years, our faces become our biographies." – *Cynthia Ozick*

fact, *n*. A disputable truth – as you see it.

"Get your facts right first and then you can distort them as much as you please." – *Mark Twain*

failure, *n*. Not the end of the road – just a detour to get you back on the right track.

"The most important thing you learn is how to fail – because most all of what you do is fail." – *Tina Fey*

fair, *adv*. Fair is cutting the piece of cake in half and letting the other person choose which half they want first. However, "let's be fair about this" means I get to cut the cake *and* choose first.

"Gravity may not be fair, but it's the law." – *Unknown*

fait accompli, *n*. Something that has been completed that is irreversible. Sexting photos that male political and sports figures sent to strangers of an asset their wives want to debit.

faith, *n*. Requirement for starting your own business when you don't know what you're doing, how to do it, or where to start. It's a belief in the possible. Your actions reflect your faith and beliefs.

"We knew we could do it. We just didn't know how we would do it." – *Danielle Lawrie, University of Washington softball fast-pitch pitcher, Player of the Year, after winning the 2009 NCAA National Championship*

false advertising, *n*. Food menu photos.

"What the hell is that!?" – *First time visitor to the Northwest shocked at the grossness and size of the geoduck placed before him by the waiter**

family picture technique, *n*. Using your immediate and extended family to land an appointment with a reluctant prospect.

"Send a photo of your favorite pet with this post-it note attached: 'I have three cats, two dogs, a gerbil, two kids, and six nephews and nieces. If you'll simply give me fifteen minutes of your time, I'll stop sending you their pictures.'" – *Jerry Hocutt*

farmer, *n*. A sales principle where the salesperson cultivates the existing customer base in hopes of getting more new business out of it, while eliminating turnover. Frowned upon by management as this is "not really selling" and full commissions shouldn't be paid. "Let's just make these house accounts and turn them over to customer service." Cf. *hunter*.

"We've migrated many of our customers into house accounts, but for some reason our churn rate is abnormally high with them. I can't understand why." – *Tampa CFO**

fate, *n*. Destiny; the inevitable adverse outcome. Malware from opening the email attachment from someone you didn't know. Salmon returning upstream.

fatigue, *n*. (Sigh) Whatever.

"God grant me the courage not to give up what I think is right, even though I think it is hopeless." – *Admiral Chester W. Nimitz*

faux, *adj*. Fake; false; a lie. "I'll get back to you."

favor, *n*. Knowing a secret that's going to pay off handsomely. A friend's form of blackmail, instigated by the victim. "Do me a favor – don't say anything to the boss about what just happened."

fax, *n*. Equipment subsidized by phone companies since they still require landlines.

fear, *n*. It's not meant to stop you, but it keeps you alert and stops you from saying and doing stupid things.

"Fear keeps you in the moment." – *Unknown*

fear of failure, *n*. Success's stop sign.

"It's impossible really means I'm afraid to fail." – *Unknown*

fear of rejection, *n*. The salesperson's greatest ally in eliminating the competition.

"The number one reason people leave the field of sales is because of their fear of rejection from cold calling." – *Frank Salisbury*

feature, *n*. In selling, the button. Sales newbies mistake the feature as the benefit customers want to buy. "Just look at the color on this 85" high def LED screen." What the customer wants to hear is, "The picture is so real it's like you're in the saddle on the Kentucky Derby winner yourself."

feedback, *n*. Honestly, no one wants it. If they get it, and agree, that means they'll have to change. And no one likes to change. So please, just keep it to yourself.

"Him: 'Wanna know what I think?' Her: 'No.'" – *Married couple**

feel, felt, found, *v*. A sales gem to create empathy with the customer and show that you're on his side. "How did you feel when Wall Street stole your life savings? I felt the same way. But I found a great new vehicle to invest your newly inherited fortune in that I know you'll love. It's called a Ponzi."

field, *n*. In sales, where the business is found, where the game is played. Ask any general manager, they'll tell you: "Get out of the office! Get into the field and find some new customers!"

"Having the world's best idea will do you no good unless you act on it. People who want milk shouldn't sit on a stool in the middle of a field in hopes that a cow will back up to them." – *Curtis Grant*

FIFO, *n*. First In First Out. Stops inventory from getting old and smelly. Similar to birth and death.

fifteen seconds, *n.pl*. Be direct. Be brief. Be gone.
"You've got fifteen seconds." – *Prospect to cold caller**

figment of the imagination, *n*. Something you want to believe is true but instinctively know it's not. "I think I nailed the interview."

FILO, *n*. First In Last Out. Leaders. Cf. *LIFO*.
"You see the biggest differences between a leader and a follower in a minefield." – *Cal FitzSimmons*

finally, *adv*. What the audience has been waiting for you to say since you started speaking.

fine, *adj*. How women end arguments. "Fine!"
"Once you are in a fight, it's too late to wonder if it was a good idea." – *Unknown*

fine print, *n*. If it was meant to be to your benefit, do you think they'd be trying to hide it like this?
"Be careful reading the fine print. There's no way you're going to like it." – *Unknown*

finger quotes, *n*. Irritating air quotes to show the speaker is sarcastically quoting someone else without realizing she looks like an idiot. Not to be confused with her one finger exclamations which mean something entirely different.

fingerprint, *n.* Every customer contact is like leaving a fingerprint behind: they're invisible, they last, and they're yours. Be careful of the impressions you leave behind.

first class, *n.* The plane's passengers whose faces you scan hoping none of them recognize you as you shuffle back to coach like a refugee.

first impression, *n.* When accurate decisions are made about you. Princeton psychologist Dr. Alex Todorov found that within 1/10 of a second of seeing your facial features, people have already made judgments about whether or not they are attracted to you, if they can trust you, how competent you are, or even if they will like you as a person.

"Intuition is the ability to come to the right conclusion when you haven't been given enough information." – *Roy H. Williams*

first offer, *n.* Not the best or last offer, but what's made to advance the conversation until both parties compromise on what works for them. "Quit throwing a tantrum buster or I'm sending you to your room."

fishing expedition, *n.* "Where were you last night?"

fix, *v.* To make it right, in your favor: "Looks like a hanging chad to me."

fixer, *n.* A chad counter.

"People who can fix things are hard to find." – *The Red Widow*

flabbergasted, *v.t.* Taken aback as incomprehensible; caught by complete surprise; totally unexpected. A meeting that starts and ends on time where something is actually accomplished.

Words That Escaped Me Before My Brain Finished Downloading

flash point, *n*. The breaking point at which someone bursts into flames. "That's it! I'm not taking this any longer! Get your stuff together and get out of my sight!" But not all mothers-in-law spontaneously combust.

fleecing, *v*. Your kids' college tuition is due.

flexibility, *n*. Illustrated by Cirque du Soleil contortionists who can make a pretzel jealous. How much you have determines how well the negotiations will go. "How much flexibility do you have?" he asked, after making the first offer. "None," she replied.

flextime, *n*. A range of hours an employee can choose to work from to get the job done. If a company doesn't offer it, employees take it anyway.

flight attendant, *n*. Tough job with a tough crowd. Cut 'em some slack.
  "Blue Moon/you saw me standing alone/without a dream in my heart/without a love of my own...." – *Southwest Airlines flight attendant with a lovely voice serenading the passengers on a delayed, late night flight out of Oakland under a bright harvest moon**

flow, *n*. To be in the moment with intense concentration. To be on a roll. "The customer was mesmerized by the salesperson's demonstration and lost all track of time." Rarely achieved but always sought. The salesperson must be alert that the flow doesn't turn south and head downhill.

flowchart, *n*. A company's hierarchical chart of management. The flow – the power – starts at the top and quickly dissipates into a trickle by the time it reaches you. At least you won't drown in power.

fly, *v*. To depart by airplane. Eventually. Maybe. You hope.

"LaGuardia Airport is like a homeless shelter for the traveler." – *Mike Barnacle on New York's airport being recognized in 2012 as the worst airport in the U.S.*

"In less than two seconds after departing the gate – two seconds! – the pilot came on the intercom and said, 'Well...you picked a great night to fly with us folks.'" – *Morning Joe host, and former Florida congressman, Joe Scarborough who, before boarding the plane in bad weather, kept telling the gate attendants that the flight should be delayed so they wouldn't have to sit on the runway. They boarded the plane anyway and immediately taxied to a waiting area where they sat for over three hours.*

focus group, *n*. Random group of people selected to tell you what they honestly think of your new service, product, or idea. Much like a family reunion except you know the people there and you don't honestly care what they think.

follow-up, *n*. What salespeople can learn from police detectives. When crimes are solved and sales are made.

"I don't know what my competitors are thinking. I've had more customers tell me I got their business simply because I followed-up as promised. I either called back, or sent the information, or just touched base by email. But for some inexplicable reason, they tell me, my competitors rarely do." – *Minneapolis saleswoman**

foot in the door, *n*. Sales expression: "If I can just get my foot in the door, I know I can make this sale." That's what keeps people out of the field of sales – they won't do what it takes to get their foot in the door.

"What attracts my attention shall have it, as I will go to the man who knocks at my door, while a thousand persons as worthy go by it, to whom I give no regard." – *Ralph Waldo Emerson*

force majeure, *n*. A contractual disclaimer inserted for an event that can't be reasonably anticipated or controlled that frees both parties from liability for non-performance. Flight get cancelled? Baggage lost? Want to sue the airlines? Check your contract for these two words and you'll see why you're flat out of luck.

"I had a straight flight from Seattle to Kansas City. How did my luggage end up in South Korea?" – *Business owner who needed his only suit for a major presentation the next day**

forecast, *n*. Crystal ball gazing. A business or sales prediction of what will happen. Really, more like what you want to happen. Not happening in either scenario.

"John sat still as the fortune-teller gazed into her crystal ball. Suddenly, she started to laugh loudly, so he leaned across and punched her on the nose. It was the first time he'd struck a happy medium." – *Allan Pease*

fork technique, *n*. A friendly warning to get the customer to return your calls or emails.

"Send the customer a fork with this note attached: 'This fork is to remind you that you *fork*-got to call me back. Don't make me come after you with a knife!'" – *Omaha saleswoman**

fraud, *n*. Bet you're looking for a picture of a Wall Street banker here, huh?

freakin' out, *v.i.* Passengers in a New York cab ride.

"My God! He nearly hit the pedestrians when he was driving on the sidewalk!" – *Panicked conversation of out-of-towners in their cab on their way back to the hotel in rush hour traffic in midtown Manhattan**

freebie, *n*. Enticement for a customer to do business with you. Bait on a hook where the fish thinks he's getting the better part of this deal.

frequent flyer, *n*. Traveler in an abusive aviation relationship.

"As you exit the plane, please make sure to gather all of your belongings. Anything left behind will be distributed evenly among the flight attendants. Please do not leave children or spouses." – *Flight attendant**

frequent flyer miles, *n*. What you try to collect without having to actually fly to get them.

"Last one off the plane must clean it." – *Pilot upon landing**

Friday, *n*. Sneak day. "I wonder if the boss will notice if I sneak away early?" She won't. She snuck out on Thursday.

fun, *n*. A good experience. Something you not only like to do, but want to do because of the challenge, excitement, or entertainment. The more fun you have, the more you do. The more you do, the quicker you learn. The quicker you learn, the better you get. An unexpected bonus: you're never discouraged when you're having fun.

"You never know. That's the fun of it." – *Patty Hewes, Damages*

function, *n*. A brain wrack. A company event you're required to attend but you're wracking your brain trying to figure how to get out of it.

"I'm sorry, I won't be able to make the picnic. My in-laws are coming to town." – *Really lame and unbelievable excuse*

funny money, *n*. Your paycheck.

"'How much do you expect to be paid?' the reporter asked. 'More than the Yankees expect to pay me.'" – *Yogi Berra*

Words That Escaped Me Before My Brain Finished Downloading

FYI, *n*. For Your Information. If in the subject line in your boss's email it means, "Get this taken care of now!" FYI in your friend's voicemail means, "Here's some juicy gossip you'll love." FYI in your college kid's text message means, "The doctors think the medicines should clear this up."

G

gaffe, *n*. An embarrassing blunder. Like when you can't tell by the voice on the phone if it's a man or a woman and you keep calling her sir.

"Coaching is eliminating mistakes before you get fired." – *Lou Holtz*

gambit, *n*. In negotiating, a calculated move to get the upper hand and throw the other party off balance. Whatever offer is made, lean back, laugh, wink, slap your thighs, and yell "That's a good one!"

game change, *n*. The tipping point. It's your response to the sales manager's question on the first job interview, "So...what do you think about cold calling?"

"I decided to hire you on that first interview when you told me, 'Cold calling sucks!' And then you continued, 'But I'm one of the best you'll ever see doing it.' I knew then that you understood cold calling and that you'd always be honest with me." – *Sales manager explaining why he hired me at his Fortune 1000 company**

game changer, *n.* Unexpected thunderstorms wreaking havoc on the airport as your plane is sitting on the taxiway, seventeenth in line for takeoff.

"I'm going out for McDonald's. Anybody want anything?" – *Passenger on flight at D/FW Airport where plane has been stranded for three hours with no food or water**

game on, *n.* Calling the other person's bluff and raising the stakes. It's like your kindergartner saying he'll run away and live with grandma if he doesn't get his way, and you packing his bags for him.

gatekeeper, *n.* The boss's bouncer who knows who to let in and what's important. It's their job to lose if they don't.

geek, *n.* The person who can relate better to your computer than to you.

"Why do we squeeze harder on the remote when we know the batteries are getting weak?" – *Unknown*

general manager, *n.* The company's field commander responsible for day-to-day operations, settling squabbles between department heads, and answering to higher-ups why the goals they set haven't been reached. In school, the principal.

get real. Earth to Congress...!

gift cards, *n.pl.* They're like extended warranties that never get used. Most people leave a dollar or two on them and never zero them out, thus they become lucrative profit centers for the issuers.

"From 2005 to 2011, an absurdly high $41 billion worth of gift cards have likely gone unredeemed." – *Wall Street Journal*

gifts, *n.pl.* It's acceptable to give them to your valued customers during the holiday season if their company's policy allows it. If you're unsure, put this note with the gift: "If you're not allowed to accept this gift as our appreciation for your business, please feel free to give it to any of your favorite charities." Congress still prefers bags of cash in small, unmarked bills – no need to wait for holidays.

give in, *v.* A nagging surrender.
"When are you going to paint the house? Today? Tomorrow? This week? You need to do it before it rains. Have you got enough paint? What about brushes? Do you need a bigger ladder?" – *What spouse hears before caving*

gloat, *v.i.* The look on the other bidders' faces when you show up five minutes too late to submit your bid for the opening.

goal, *n.* A goal is like getting a good night's sleep: it's something you want – even need – but that doesn't mean you're going to get it.
"Scientists have found that urine – urine! – can generate enough energy to charge your cell phone. Well then, in that case I get up three times a night to charge my phone." – *David Letterman*
"On this team, we're all united in a common goal: to keep my job." – *Lou Holtz*
"Our guest of honor is living proof that having a goal, a dream, and struggling hard to attain it, don't always work." – *Unknown*

gobbledygook, *n.* Geek speak.

going postal, *n.* Not your mail. Happens at unforeseen exit interviews.

golden parachute, *n*. Ridiculously insane wads of cash thrown at high flying executives to provide a cushy landing when the board unexpectedly triggers the ejection button. When regular employees are pushed out the exit door they're given a ball of twine, paper, two balsa sticks and told to "go fly a kite".

golden rule, *n*. In religion, "Whatever you wish that men would do to you, do so to them." In business, "He who has the gold makes the rules." In politics, "Craft your laws to favor those who fill your war chests with gold."

"Kindness is the language which the deaf can hear and the blind can see." – *Mark Twain*

golf, *n*. Where important business is discussed; too important to invite you to be in the foursome. To win at golf you must lose to the boss, helping everyone to come in under par.

"He likes to be alone in the woods, go places where few have gone before and face seemingly impossible challenges. Unfortunately, he does all this while golfing." – *Unknown*

good cop/bad cop, *n*. Negotiating game made popular by FBI interrogators and used in other professions. Salesperson to customer: "I'll go to bat for you. I want you to get the best part of this deal. But my vice president is a real SOB. What he'll want in return for a better price is full payment upfront and no net 30." First surgeon: "You're going to die." Second surgeon, the next day: "You'll be okay, but it's going to cost you $280,000 to remove that ingrown toenail."

good enough. After recovering from the shock of seeing the recent college tuition hikes, what you tell your new high school grad about his education.

"Life would be so simple if our biggest problems came when we were fresh out of high school and knew everything." – *Unknown*

good luck. Encouragement given to others when the odds are stacked against them. Two words that first-time parents hear from the hospital staff as they're leaving with their newborn.

"How do you say 'Good luck' in Apache?" asked Jesse Stone. "Go get 'em, kemosabe," replied Indian "Crow" Cromartie. – *Robert B. Parker*

good news/bad news, *n*. Your company's annual flu shot where the bad news is delivered first. Ouch!

"The absence of bad news doesn't always mean good news." – *The Good Wife*

goof-up, *v*. Screw up that won't necessarily get you fired and could possibly start a new industry. The 3M employee who was trying to make a stickier glue, but ended up making Post-It notes. The luxury hotel chef in Saratoga Springs, New York, who tried to insult a guest who was unhappy with his food and accidentally created the potato chip, which the guest loved.

Google, *n*. Replaces mom and dad who always had all the answers.

"Google it." – *Dad to 5th grader*

"It's no longer what you know. Google has all the answers. Today, it's what you do with what you know." – *Thomas Friedman*

Google ads, *n.pl*. Money printing machine for a company with a catchy name. Requires Ph.D. to figure out how to make them pay off.

got a minute, *n*. Never good. Three words bosses don't like to hear. It will take more than a minute, or it's about a co-worker conflict, or a major account has just tanked.

"I have had more trouble with D.L. Moody than with any other man I ever met." – *D.L. Moody*

go-to guy, *n*. Tonto.

"Intellectual: someone who can listen to Rossini's 'William Tell Overture' without thinking of the Lone Ranger." – *Billy Connolly*

GPS, *n*. Directions for lost souls. Thank you God.

"I just got lost in thought. It was unfamiliar territory." – *Unknown*

greed, *n*. Chum for Wall Street sharks.

gridlock, *n*. Rubik's cube, on wheels, in rush hour.

guarantee, *n*. The reason companies can give a "guaranteed or your money back" promise is because of the "endowment effect": once the customer possesses the product, even for a few minutes, he feels it "belongs" to him and he'll refuse to give it up. Doesn't work with services because you can't take back what they now know or have used.

guerilla marketing, *n*. Creative marketing by starving entrepreneurs when they don't have the money, resources, and manpower.

"I tried promoting our Thanksgiving special by taking a bunch of turkeys up in a plane and releasing them to fly over the city to get peoples' attention. I didn't know turkeys can't fly." – *Fictional WKRP Cincinnati station owner (even bad guerilla marketing ideas are memorable)*

guess again. Not even close.

guru, *n*. There are no gurus with life's answers. Look for people who will ask you the tough questions so you can find your own answers.

"You don't seem to be happy in your job here. If you could do anything in the world – anything – what would you really want to do with your life?" – *Business owner to employee who quickly found his calling, quit his job, and started his own successful business**

gut check, *n*. Instinct's alarm bell. A queasy feeling in the pit of the stomach, usually right. What fishermen do when cleaning their catch.

"I don't rely a whole lot on my gut." – *Arizona Governor Jan Brewer to CNN when pressed on her initial reaction to the state legislature passing the 2014 Senate Bill 1062 allowing businesses to refuse service to customers (e.g. LGBT) if it is against the company's religious beliefs; she vetoed the bill days later after a fierce backlash from state and national business leaders and an intense firestorm of national ridicule*

"It is through science that we prove, but through intuition that we discover." – *Henri Poincare*

guts, *n*. A challenge to manhood: "You don't have the guts to say that to the boss." You do. You say it. You're fired.

H

habit, *n*. Three types of habits: good, bad, and nasty; unless you count a nun's habit, so that makes four. It takes twenty-one days to form a habit, and an eternity to break.

"I was sorry to have my name mentioned as one of the great authors, because they have a sad habit of dying off. Chaucer is dead, Spenser is dead, so is Milton, so is Shakespeare, and I'm not feeling so well myself." – *Mark Twain*

haggle, *v*. To barter, negotiate. At an American business lunch hosted by the CFO, the only haggling is between the CFO and himself: "Should I leave a 10% tip or is 7% good enough?"

"What's mine is mine. What's yours is negotiable." – *Charlie Cook*

half-hand handshake, *n*. Shaking hands while holding on weakly to the other person's finger-tips; a.k.a. "kiss the queen's hand" handshake. Used by royalty and those who think they are, who don't want to touch you and want you to keep your distance. They're silently thinking, "Back off, Jack!" accompanied by a tight-lip smile and beady little eyes. The half-hand means that person is uncomfortable with you. If you're greeted this way, once you release hands, take a step back to give them their space, and then put your hands behind your back to show them you have no weapons.

"A handshake can't be forced on someone who is not quite ready to come to grips." – *Maureen Dowd*

hand-holding, *n*. Coddling the newbie until she gets the gist of it. Some companies think two weeks of sales training for someone who has never sold before should do it. The same time it takes to master golf.

handwriting, *n*. Brain writing; visual evidence of why we're in the sorry state we're in.

"I showed one of our salesmen a brief note written by a prospect I was to meet outside the office and he warned me that the man's writing indicated that he may be violent and to only meet him in our office. During the office interview the prospect told me he had recently been paroled from the state penitentiary for what turned out to be a violent crime." – *Saleswoman telling sales manager about the timely warning she got from a co-worker who studied handwriting analysis**

happy, *adj*. You'll always be happy if you're having fun.

"I'm happy when I pitch (do my job) well so I only do things that help me be happy." – *Tom Seaver, Hall of Fame pitcher inducted by the highest percentage ever recorded (98.84%)*

happy campers, *n.pl*. It's that couple you saw checking in at the Marriott who had their bus-size RV and towed Humvee being parked by the valet before heading to their suite.

harass, *v.t*. Popular management technique used to motivate employees to be on time for meetings. Used by unhappy customers on their salespeople when the delivery deadline of their product has been missed again. A popular touchy-feely game practiced with great vigor in Congress.

"We have an awful lot of members who don't understand that harass is one word, not two." – *Former Colorado Congresswoman Pat Schroeder*

hard sell, *n*. Infomercials. But wait! There's more!

headhunters, *n.pl*. Sales recruiters who try to find you a better job – unless it's one they'd rather have and take it first.
"When I saw this job come up, I interviewed for it myself and got it." – *Branch manager telling her new salespeople how she found the job when she was a sales recruiter**

headlines, *n. pl*. What you give to Driver personalities when talking with them. Save the details for the Analyticals.

headquarters, *n*. Working at corporate is like watching a Broadway play while sitting in the front row – lots of drama, comedy, and intrigue.
"In four years we went through sixteen sales managers, general managers, vice presidents, and presidents in our one location and division alone, all of whom were either fired, or demoted and transferred to remote areas of the country. Not one was ever promoted. And that's not counting over seventy salespeople who were fired or quit." – *Jerry Hocutt*

health insurance, *n*. What every Congressional member wants, needs, and has – at a very favorable premium. What they think is a luxury the working class doesn't need and should quit complaining about.
"Let them eat cake." – *Marie Antoinette, oblivious to the condition of the peasants and the fact that they couldn't afford the ingredients for cake, as she stroked the blue Hope diamond gracing her neck (before she lost both of them – her neck and the diamond)*

hear, *v.* Confused with "listen" and "understand". For example, the prospect mentions how well the trial is going with the competitor's products, and the salesperson reports back to the sales manager that the prospect had no objections and the sale looks like a lock.

"Knowing something and understanding it are not the same thing." *–Mitch Albom*

here's the thing. Uh-oh.

Hershey kiss technique, *n.* Send an infant's shoe with a Hershey kiss inside to your prospect with this note: "It would be sweet to get my foot in the door."

"I sent fifteen shoes to my prospects the week after your seminar and got five appointments from them the following week." *– Testimonial from the owner of a print shop in New Jersey**

hidden need, *n.* What the customer is not telling the salesperson because the knowledge would put her at a disadvantage in negotiations.

"Don't let the salesman know our refrigerator caught on fire. Play it cool and maybe we can ice this deal in our favor." *– Wife to husband**

hierarchy, *n.* The company's status of people from top to bottom, from most important to least important. If you don't know where you fit, then you know.

high pressure selling, *n.* It's kicked off when the car salesman asks for your keys to show his sales manager that you're serious about buying.

"Once the car salesman asked me for my keys, I told him I was on to his tricks and wouldn't put up with it and left. He literally came running after me, but I told him he had his chance and he blew it." *– New college grad looking to buy her first new car now that she could afford it**

higher authority, *n*. A negotiating technique that makes you look like the good guy in the negotiating process while making a third, inaccessible party the bad guy. It removes you as the final decision maker who can't grant every concession the other party wants. It slows the negotiations down and frustrates the prospect so much she'll ask for fewer concessions later. It's the car salesman who has to keep going back to the sales manager for approvals to the changes you want to make. If you're a one-man shop without a higher authority, invent one by telling the buyer, "I'll have to take it to my investors, but they'll want something in return." An investor can be your spouse, partner, aunt, uncle, kid, neighbor, or anyone who's loaned you a buck for your business.

hindsight is 20/20. Business myopia. Phrase made popular by governmental agencies for letting the bid go to the lowest bidder on another billion dollar cost overrun project that will come in two years late. Will be blindly repeated on the next bid anyway.

hokey, *adj*. Corny. Not an Arkansas mispronunciation for hockey.
    "Your tongue will slap your brain silly." – *South Carolina barbeque pit master pitching his ribs*
    "The inventor of the hokey-pokey has died. That is going to be one long burial." – *Stephen Colbert*

holidays, *n.pl*. The days you work from home.

holy grail of sales, *n*. Never cold call again. An illusion. Wishful thinking.

home based business, *n*. The White House.

homework, *n*. The process of discovery: what you know, what you don't know, and what you're looking for. "What is that! Where did it come from? How big is it? Are those teeth? Is it poisonous? Will it bite? Catch it and get it out of here!"

honestly, *adv.* A statement meant to show candidness, but leaving a little fudge room. "Honestly, I didn't know that was your customer" means "I wasn't for sure when I made the sale, and I didn't want to ask so I could say, 'I honestly didn't know'."

"What I'm trying to do is be as honest as I can. And I don't normally do that." – *Fired Washington Redskins head coach Mike Shanahan*

honesty, *n.* Truth that can hurt. Husband to wife: "I accidentally put your jeans on by mistake. They fit perfectly!"

"There's nothing that can discourage people as much as honesty." – *Henning Mankell*

hook, *n.* In fishing a small, sharp pointed object hidden by appealing bait that reels the fish in. Same in sales.

"You've got to hide the hook with the bait so you can fool the fish. They're smart little critters." – *Grandma Annie**

hope, *n.* FIFO when starting a risky new venture.

"I'm doing better since I've given up hope." – *Robert B. Parker*

"To be a Mariners fan is to have the hope beaten out of you." – *Seattle Times sports columnist Larry Stone on the Mariners opening day March 31, 2014*

horizontal marketing, *n.* Looking and working for referrals to different departments and branches within your customer's large company. Cf. *vertical market*.

hot button, *n.* The customer's turn-on that is frustratingly hard to find. But watch their body language. It can reveal what moves them when their words won't.

"If the customer suddenly unfolds his arms, uncrosses his legs, leans forward, exposes the palms of his hands, and starts asking questions, you've hit his hot button." – *Seattle psychologist**

hot potato, *n*. A problem you throw to others, hoping they won't throw it back. But problems can be very good for business, since solving them is the business you're in.

hot seat, *n*. Take a seat. We have some questions.

hotel, *n*. Home, home on the road. (Sung to the tune of "Home on the Range".) Easy to make reservations. Unfortunately, not easy for hotels to keep because "the other party never checked out, and under the law we can't evict them." Some have bedbug populations they encourage you to pack up and take home with you, their treat. Plenty of free reading material and snacks located under every bed. Plus, housekeeping has set the radio clock alarm for 4 a.m. to surprise you and get your day started. You can't miss it – the volume has been turned up full blast.

house accounts, *n.pl.* The comptroller's brilliant idea for how to cut costs and avoid paying commissions with the belief that "once a customer, a customer for life – because we're so awesome."

HOV lanes, *n.pl.* Some single car drivers consider them as their personal passing lanes.
"I was just trying to go around the slow traffic officer. I was running late for an appointment." – *Driver who pulled out of her lane on a blind curve and into the HOV lane only to rear end a vehicle stopped in the lane with engine problems**

how, *n*. The second most valuable employee is the one who knows "how". The most valuable employee knows how, and then does it.
"The work will teach you how to do it." – *Estonian proverb*

however, *conj*. Used to clarify what was first thought to be a compliment into what was really meant. "I really like you a lot; however, I never want to see you again. But feel free to follow me on my social networks."

hubris, *n*. Narcissism; braggadocio; self-centered; self-promoting; exaggerated pride. It's the attention addicted, sex-scandal prone politicos who resign from office after being exposed, only to come back in a couple of years feigning humility in order to gain forgiveness to recoup their power.

"(Failed New York City mayoral candidate Anthony) Weiner finished with a tiny 5 percent of the vote, and just after his concession speech, he gave a fitting goodbye to the reporters who covered his campaign as cameras caught him flipping off a journalist." – *Politico*

human resources, *n*. HR. Formerly the personnel department. Best known as the hiring, firing, and "get your act together or else" department. Gatekeeper of résumés. Distributor of exit interviews.

"HR director: 'What is your greatest weakness?' Applicant: 'Honesty.' HR director: 'I don't think honesty is a weakness.' Applicant: 'I don't give a damn what you think.'" – *Unknown*

humor, *n*. The truth sneaking up on tiptoes.

"Humor can be marvelously therapeutic. It can deflate without destroying; it can instruct while it entertains; it saves us from our pretensions; and it provides an outlet for feelings that expressed another way would be corrosive." – *George Valliant*

hump day, *n*. Wednesday that's a Friday for too many.

hunter, *n*. Aggressive salesperson who finds new business instead of waiting for the business to find her. Not a favorite of the farmer salespeople who sit around the office waiting to be found.

"Farmer to female hunter: Ok, lady! OK! It's a deer. Just let me get my saddle off of it!" – *Unknown*

hype, *n*. The sizzle before the fizzle.

Words That Escaped Me Before My Brain Finished Downloading

"If you want a crowd, start a fight." – *P.T. Barnum who would stage fights in towns to draw crowds and then hand out circus tickets*

hyperbole, *n.* Given to great exaggeration. Much ado about nothing. Most common displays are in TV news programs: "Breaking News!"; "This Just In!" It's like getting an email where the sender uses all caps and you want to reply, "STOP SCREAMING AT ME!"

hypnotic trance, *n.* What talking on your cell phone put you in when you were driving. Why you had the accident. Why you got the ticket. Why your car insurance is going up. Hope the call was important.

hypnotism, *n.* Subliminal persuasion. It's the voices in your head convincing you that there's better things to do than whatever it is you're supposed to be doing because you don't want to do it. Like making those calls you've been putting off all morning.

hypnotist, *n.* A salesperson of beliefs.

I

I got this. Relax. This is in my wheelhouse. Inscribed on the tombstone of the captain of the Titanic.

I said so. How bosses and parents end arguments.

I was wrong. Wha...? Wow! That's a first. What women dream men will someday say. Don't hold your breath.

idea, *n*. A thought that seemed good at the time. Why second thoughts are better.
   "Bat day seems like a good idea, but I question the advisability of giving bats in the Bronx to 40,000 Yankee fans." – *Aaron Bacall*

identity theft, *n*. When you spend the next five years trying to prove you are who you say you are.

if I could show you. Popular phrase used by some salespeople to trap the customer into buying. What you don't want to see from your Yoga partner in front of you doing the downward facing dog.

illusion, *n*. A pay raise with more take-home money.

"Teach your children about taxes. Eat 30% of their ice cream." – *Unknown*

I'm sorry. The best pick-up line men can use because women seldom hear it.

image, *n*. A salesperson's tool to get the customer to feel as if he's already made the purchase. "Imagine if you will, diving off the island's thirty-foot waterfall cliff into the deep blue pool below," the travel agent gushes. Instead, the tourist sees his head bashing onto a hidden boulder, and the water gurgling red flotsam. Some images just create themselves.

impasse, *n*. A staring contest in negotiations. It's where both sides want what the other side won't give. The best way to break the impasse is to offer something new the other side may not have considered – with conditions. "I can't give you a higher guaranteed salary," the team owner says, "but I can give you incentive bonuses that will surpass your current salary if certain conditions are met." Of course, the conditions are rigged and can never be met.

impatient, *adj*. The single driver in the two-person carpool lane in rush hour traffic, with inflatable Wanda strapped into the passenger seat beside him.

"Who's your friend?" – *State trooper*

imperfect, *adj*. What makes the common rare and sought after; like the 1955-S double die penny, or the 1918 Inverted Jenny stamp.

"It's the imperfections that give you personality." – *Dave Grohl*

implementation plan, *n*. It's like an incentive plan agreed upon between the employer and employee to make sure things are on track to go smoothly: "Get busy or you're fired!"

"Abel, put that camera down right now! Abel, you're fired. Out!" – *CEO Tim Armstrong firing AOL's creative director for their Patch local-news business in front of a room full of employees, and while on a conference call with a thousand other employees listening in (Bloomberg, August 13, 2013)*

implicate, *v.t.* It was that girl in class taking the make-up exam raising her hand and telling the teacher she thought someone was "copying me." And you're the only two in the class taking the exam.

implication, *n.* Incriminating involvement by innuendo. "Saw my competitors at the circus the other day. Didn't know so many could fit into such a tiny little car."
"I had a friend who was a clown. When he died, all his friends went to the funeral in one car." – *Steven Wright*

implied warranty, *n.* "You promised!" Verbal guarantee based on trust, sealed with a handshake and a wink that says, "Chump!"

imply, *v.t.* To insinuate as being true, to be a fact. "I don't want to say that your offer is – like you – insane, but...."
"When it's true it doesn't need to be said." – *Tina Fey*

impossible, *adj.* That's what I do.
"Why not you?" – *Seattle Seahawk's quarterback Russell Wilson's dad's advice to him as a youngster; and what he challenged his teammates with "Why not us?" as he led his team to win Super Bowl XLVIII in just his second year (and the most-watched television event in U.S. history, February 2, 2014)*

impressive, *adj.* Awesome, but short of good enough. "I was blown away with your presentation! But we're going with your competitor instead."

improve, *v.* Keep looking. There's always a better, faster, easier, more efficient way to do whatever you're doing.

"No matter how old a mother is, she still watches her middle-aged children for signs of improvement." – *Florida Scott-Maxwell*

improvisation, *n.* Jazz. Making it up as you go, because you have no idea where events will lead. Happens on every interview, cold call, and negotiation.

"How does an improvisational jazz ensemble know when the piece is finished?" – *Jerry Hocutt*

improvise, *v.* I'll think of something.

impulse buying, *v.t.* Sure. Why not?

in a nutshell. Why didn't you say so in the first place? What took you so long to get here?

in conclusion. Thank God!

"If your primary chute doesn't open, and the reserve chute doesn't open either, well, that's what you call jumping to a conclusion." – *Unknown*

indicators, *n.pl.* Clues about what is likely to happen. You don't need to be clairvoyant to decipher them.

"The customer hasn't been taking or returning my calls or emails about our new price increases. I wonder what this means?" – *Saleswoman worried about losing her account**

indictment, *n.* An indication from the grand jury that the manufacturer didn't put all the right parts into the product before sending it to market.

indirect, *adj*. Passive-aggressive; a different way of getting to the same place without a direct confrontation. "I hope you have a job lined up if you fail to keep another appointment with your customers."

influence, *n*. The power of persuasion. The ability to convince others of your point of view. Doesn't mean you're right. Just that you have the clout to get others to go along with the program.

influencer, *n*. Not the decision maker, but one who tells the decision maker what to decide (wife, partner, executive assistant).

information, *n*. Knowledge that was previously unknown, often to the surprise of the receiver. "Why is your car being towed?"
    "Information is the currency of democracy." – *Ralph Nader*

information overload, *n*. Blown brain fuse. (Don't) tell me more.

initiate, *v.t*. The car's starter. You're not going anywhere until you get started.
    "My grandmother started walking five miles a day when she was sixty. She's ninety-seven now, and we don't know where the hell she is." – *Ellen DeGeneres*

inner circle, *n*. A company's business clique at the highest level that meets in secret and denies its existence, much like the Illuminati, Knights Templar, and Opus Dei.

innuendo, *n*. To leapfrog ahead on the promotion list ask the boss, "What did Shirley blow on the breathalyzer when she was pulled over last night?"

inquiries, *n.pl*. Requested information from prospective buyers. Sometimes by the police. Nothing to worry about as long as you have an alibi.

insane, *adj.* Salespeople who love cold calling.
"I became insane with long intervals of horrible sanity." – *Edgar Allan Poe*

inside salespeople, *n.* Outside salespeople going nowhere.

insight, *n.* I heard what you said, but I also know what you meant.
"Listen for the meanings – not the words." – *Bill Moyers*

insurance, *n.* A legalized gambling industry glad to take your premiums but reluctant to pay off the bet when they lose. Your Bronx bookie, Al "Three Fingers" Diablo, is better at paying his bets.
"We've had to triple your premiums because you filed a claim which we had to pay." – *Letter from insurance company justifying their increase because of a first-time claim**

intangible, *adj.* Something you can't put your finger on but have a feeling is there.
"How do you know there is wind? Gravity? God? You look for the effects." – *House, M.D.*

integration meeting, *n.* Company code for a meeting to discuss the new merger and pending layoffs. It's like NFL draft day where you hope you don't end up with the undrafted free agents.
"When I played pro football, I never set out to hurt anyone deliberately – unless it was, you know, important, like a league game or something." – *Dick Butkus*

integrity, *n.* A character witness.
"Once you give up integrity, the rest is a piece of cake." – *J.R. Ewing*

intellectual conversation, *n.* An impotent discussion about doing the right thing, but then taking no action to do it; conversations on gun control, climate change, education, debt limits, spending.

intelligence, *n.* The barter of spies.
"Intelligence is mainly a failure business." *–Rubicon*

intense, *adj.* Sitting on pins and needles. After making an emergency landing at a small, remote airport, being told by the pilot that because the jet is so heavy with fuel and passengers, that he's waiting for clearance from the FAA liaison to see if the plane can lift off the shortened runway. Really intense: the jet screaming down the runway on takeoff and holding your breath the FAA and pilot made the right calculations.

intern, *n.* A clever way to hire someone without pay or benefits in exchange for college credits while calling it a "life experience you'll always be thankful for." If the worker falls for this, he's in the right place.
"I know what it's like to be an intern, to work without pay and to be abused. I'm a mom." – *Unknown*

interruption, *n.* The pin in a windbag.
"The more he talks, the less he actually says." – *Former Prime Minister Gordon Brown*

interview, *n.* A date to see if it leads to marriage. Whether it's a job or sales interview, the parties are often unprepared even though they've had ample time.
"I asked the job applicant to bring a résumé and two references. He arrived with the résumé – and two people." – *Seattle Times*

intimidate, *v.t.* The New Zealand "Ka Mate" Haka (Maori war cry) performed before soccer and rugby matches.
"The first and great commandment is, don't let them scare you." – *Elmer Davis*

introduce, *v.t.* To make the unknown, known. Okay with people. Not so much with diseases.

introvert, *n.* Don't talk to me. Leave me alone.
   "You might be an introvert if you enjoyed time-out as a kid; if your favorite game is solitaire; you can't understand what's so bad about solitary confinement; and you avoid buying new clothes so people won't comment on them." – *Thom S. Rainier*

inventory, *n.* What you have in stock the customer doesn't want. What you don't have in stock that the customer wants.

invest, *v.t.* To gamble with hopes of getting a greater return than what you put in. Brokers use *invest* instead of *cost*, since cost rhymes with loss.

investment, *n.* Slot machines are the most honest investments: you understand how they work, you know they're rigged, and you understand you'll lose more than you win. But with slot machines you still have hope.
   "Why would you invest with a Wall Street broker who rides the subway to work?" – *Warren Buffett*

investors, *n.pl.* People who have more money than ideas.
   "Getting an idea should be like sitting down on a pin; it should make you jump up and do something." – *E.I. Simpson*

IRS, *n.* A very taxing federal agency using rules even the auditors admit they don't comprehend. Trying to arrive at an amicable compromise on monies owed by its citizens and small businesses, the IRS follows the same federal guidelines used in negotiating with terrorists – don't do it. Meanwhile, over two dozen Fortune 500 companies paid no federal income taxes over the past four years. (This last statement will be true regardless of which year you read this.)

"Boeing's 2013 Federal Tax Refund: $199 Million." – Seattle Times headline (March 2, 2014) showing that not only did Boeing pay no income taxes on $5.9 billion in profits, but over the past twelve years they have accumulated refunds of $1.6 billion; once again, every citizen paid more in income taxes than Boeing

IRS audit, *n.* Job security for legions of federal employees. Primary purpose of audits is so you'll tell your friends you're being audited, thus scare them straight so they'll never try to take legitimate deductions. Next to owning the U.S. Mint and printing their own money, the government's main source of work to create a steady, year-round cash flow.

"If we had a simple, one page tax form that could be understood by a twelve-year old, do you know how many people you'd put out of work?" – *CPA and tax consultant**

is it true. A question to find out if it's a lie. If the answer is "yes", then it's a lie. "Is it true this is the best you can do?"

"If you believe it, is it true?" – *Jerry Hocutt*

it factor, *n.* Something someone has without knowing they have it or how they got it; something that everyone else sees but they don't. Much like a plumber's crack.

J

jingle, *n*. A catchy phrase marketing departments devise for kids who still ride in their car seats so they'll keep singing it to drive their parents over the edge. "Look mom! The golden arches," the toddler screams. "Dah-dah-ta-dah. I'm lovin' it!"

job applicant, *n*. What you graduate to with your new diploma. A feeling of hopelessness.
 "I asked the applicant why she wanted to be in sales. She replied, 'I want to impress my 'crush'." – *Jerry Hocutt*

job creator, *n*. Problems.

job fair, *n*. It's speed dating with a résumé. In Hollywood, actors call them "cattle calls". In either case, you're hoping the mass, micro-auditions lead to a callback.

job interview, *n*. An audition where first impressions could be your last. Most are over in minutes without the applicant even being aware of it. Responses that guarantee you won't be invited back for the second interview: "I want to go into sales until I find myself." "I figure I have to start somewhere." "Do you have anger management classes?"

"Eight percent of recent college grads brought their parents along to a job interview. What's more, a full three percent actually had their parents sit in on their job tryout." – *Adecco 2013 survey*

job search, *n.* Looking for Sasquatch. An exercise in humility and frustration.

jobs, *n.pl.* Two are needed to pay the bills. Three if you have student loans.
"You do your job. You'll figure it out." – *Robert B. Parker*

judgments, *n.pl.* Opinions best kept to yourself, even when asked.
"The pants are fine. It's your butt that makes you look fat." – *Judy Carter*
"Good judgment comes from experience, and a lot of that comes from bad judgment." – *Unknown*

K

Karma, *n.* Payback. What your parents wished for.

"True terror is to wake up one morning and discover that your high school class is running the country." – *Kurt Vonnegut*

key man insurance, *n.* Insurance taken out by partners on partners to protect their business in case of the other's death. Partners then begin discreet Google search for "made" men from Kansas City.

key players, *n.pl.* They're like the Supreme Court justices: each has an equal vote, and each is a part of the majority or minority factions; one may be the swing and deciding vote. Find and appeal to the swing voter.

"You said that if the other high school principal would do business with me, then you would too. Here's his signed contract. Have we got a deal?" – *Texas school picture photographer getting the second high school principal's business**

keynote speaker, *n.* Event speaker brought in to national conventions to motivate the troops and add levity, before the hammer falls by executive management on what went wrong this past year.

"Speaker: 'I have only ten minutes and hardly know where to begin.' Voice at the back: 'Begin at the ninth.'" – *Jacob Braude*

The Wickedly Fun Dictionary of Business

kick-ass, *adj*. How the boss motivates the smart-ass, dumbass, badass, wiseass, and kiss-ass.

"I don't want to hurt you, but it is on my list." – *Brad Thor*

kickback, *n*. Bribes paid to land lucrative contracts or to take shortcuts in completing the contract with inferior parts and construction. Congress calls them campaign donations, born from pork barrel projects in their districts. For example, providing $500 million in new M-1 Abrams tanks to the army that says they don't need them and they don't want them. Tough! You're getting them.

kids, *n.pl*. Advertisers' unpaid sales interns. They tell their parents what to buy.

"If you came home and found a strange man teaching your kids to punch each other, or trying to sell them all kinds of products, you'd kick him right out of the house, but here you are; you come in and the TV is on, and you don't think twice about it." – *Jerome Singer*

kiosks, *n.pl*. Mall bazaars.

KISG, *n*. Keep It Simple Grandma. The salesperson's barometer of their true sales skills.

"You cannot really understand something unless you can explain it to your grandmother." – *Unknown*

Kismet, *n*. Fate. He saw the "No Solicitors" sign on the door but went in anyway, and then came face-to-face with Kismet.

"Sometimes I lie awake at night and I ask, 'Why me?' And the voice says, 'Nothing personal, your name just happened to come up.'" – *Charlie Brown*

KISS, *n*. Keep It Simple Stupid. Has led to many successful sexual harassment lawsuits when not fully understood by the opposite sex. "Let's KISS."

"I wasn't kissing your daughter, sir – I was just whispering in her mouth." – *Chico Marx*

kiss off, *v.t.* The subject line on your email from your last job interview.

know, *v.* False presumption of the answer. "I *know* you! I remember your face, but I can't recall your name."

"Nothing is exciting if you know what the outcome is going to be." – *Northern Exposure*

knowing, *adj.* Having knowledge or information, preferably others don't know you have. "Knowing the competitor was a weasel, it was easy to bait the trap."

"I knew everything I was ever going to know. But I didn't know that I knew it." – *Lee Child*

kooks, *n.pl.* Thanks social media for exposing them.

"The voices in my head may not be real, but they have some good ideas." – *Unknown*

kudos, *n.* A backhanded congratulatory remark made to someone you didn't think would be able to pull it off. What you don't want to hear over the plane's intercom upon landing: "Kudos to our First Officer who just made his first successful landing by himself!" (Yikes! He's had unsuccessful ones?)

"A good landing is any landing you can walk away from." – *Official U.S. Air Force dictionary definition**

Kumbaya, *n.* A song of infinite verses and of togetherness sang around the campfire or around the coffeemaker at work. More of a sing-song prayer that "we'll get our act together before it's too late" kind of togetherness.

L

laissez-faire, *n*. Business to government: "Bug off!"

last impression, *n*. The first impression gets you noticed. The last one gets engraved on your tombstone.
    "Looked up the elevator shaft to see if the car was on the way down. It was." – *On the tombstone of 39-year old Harry Edsel Smith, Albany, New York*

laughter, *n*. Bwa-Ha-Ha-Ha coming from HR where they're reviewing the latest batch of résumés.
    "Am a perfectionist and rarely if if ever forget details." – *Fortune magazine, actual comment on résumé*

law of reciprocation, *n*. Psychological tool of influence: if you give someone something, they feel obligated to return the favor – perhaps giving something of even more value.
    "Here, take my scarf. Oh! Can I have your boots?" – *Sister to sister*

layoff notices, *n.pl*. The good news is you didn't get one on this round. The bad news is they're adding your co-worker's workload to yours but not her pay.

layoffs, *n.pl.* Putting everyone in the same boat before pulling the plug.

lead generation, *n.* A dead-end list of unqualified prospects the marketing department drummed up that's only interested in getting the promised free gift – not in having an appointment or in buying anything.

leader, *n.* That's the person going on with or without you.
"In the simplest terms, a leader is one who knows where he wants to go, and gets up and goes." – *John Erskine*

leadership, *n.* Taking action while others debate and seek consensus.
"I can honestly say that I was never affected by the question of the success of an undertaking. If I felt it was the right thing to do, I was for it regardless of the possible outcome." – *Golda Meir*

leading question, *n.* What the attorney can't ask a witness on direct examination, as she'll be seen as suggesting the answer she wants the witness to give. But okay to use by salespeople, even though the police call it entrapment.
"Wouldn't you rather have a live band at the reception instead of a DJ and recorded music?" – *Wedding planner*

leap of faith, *n.* Belief that once you start a scary undertaking something will happen to help you find your way. It's Indiana Jones in the *Last Crusade* holding his breath and stepping into the abyss to cross over to find the Holy Grail when a footbridge miraculously appears to save him from plunging to his death.
"If you have real internal faith, you have greater power than anyone else." – *Chris Matthews*

learn, *v.* To finally understand, either voluntarily or involuntarily.

"We're going to operate a certain way, and if you're not, we're not changing our standard for your actions." – *University of Washington football coach Chris Petersen on how he handles discipline with his players*

learning curve, *n.* It's how fast you can learn so you can take the training wheels off. In baseball, one breaking ball to the head and you'll be ahead of the curve.

"To know the road ahead, ask those coming back." – *Chinese proverb*

leave behind, *n.* A sample of the product left with the prospect to create guilt, setting up the law of reciprocation (an obligation to return a favor given). "I'll leave you this sample and call next week to see what you think." The two obligations created are that the prospect will take the call next week, and that she will have a decision. Actually works very well if you have the courage to call back.

leg up, *n.* The first one out of the starting blocks, though not necessarily the projected winner.

"We need to get the first appointment with the prospect before the competitors do so we can establish the decision-making criteria." – *Company owner to sales team**

legitimate, *adj.* Valid complaint by the offended. "I have a legitimate gripe with you!" Seen by the gripee as illegitimate. The bastard!

lemon, *n.* Defective product waiting to be squeezed by a lawsuit. Get enough lemons and you have a class action lemonade lawsuit.

lemon law, *n.* Consumer protection against lemons. As class action lawyers say, "That sucks!"

let me finish. Aggressive statement finished off with an exclamation point, squinty eyes, pounding fist, and a raised voice to someone who doesn't want to hear the answer.

"Let me finish, Senator!" – *Witness turning hostile to Senate committee member during inquiry*

letter, *n*. Evidence of what you're thinking.

"I'm sorry about the long letter. I didn't have time to write a short one." – *Pascal*

"A sentence should contain no unnecessary words, a paragraph no unnecessary sentences, for the same reason that a drawing should have no unnecessary lines and a machine no unnecessary parts. This requires not that the writer make all sentences short, or avoid all detail and treat subjects only in outline, but that every word tell." – *William Strunk, Jr.*

leverage, *n*. Having something on the other person where you can exploit their weakness to your advantage. It's knowing your only competitor backed out of the competition to get the business while not letting the customer know you know.

"An interpreter is one who enables two persons of different languages to understand each other by repeating to each what it would have been to the interpreter's advantage for the other to have said." – *Ambrose Bierce*

liability, *n*. A defective product (car brakes, drugs, toys) that's going to make a cushy living for lawyers. Sought out by lawyers in every manufactured product. And it doesn't have to be a real liability, just as long as it looks like one.

lie, *v*. Where the truth is buried. "The new sports arena won't cost the public a dime," boasted the billionaire basketball owners.

"Lying fixes everything." – *Louis C.K.*

life insurance, *n*. You're betting you'll die. The insurance company is betting you won't. Either way you lose.

"Of course, as you get older your premiums will increase because we know you're going to die." – *Insurance salesman**

LIFO, *n*. Last In First Out. Followers. Cf. *FILO*.

like, *v*. A gut feeling of trust. Nothing is bought or sold absent the likability factor – unless there is no other choice.

"I could never learn to like her – except on a raft at sea with no other provisions in sight." – *Mark Twain*

likely, *adj*. Probability of happening. "Think we'll get sued if they find we're substituting horse meat in the meatballs?" Likely.

limited liability, *n*. Two vague words in small print that void any warranties in the contract and say it's your fault. It's when you have hurricane coverage but the insurance company says your house was destroyed by flood waters and not wind damage. Dummy! You should have purchased flood insurance (which no one sells since you actually live near the water).

line in the sand, *n*. Made famous by the 26-year old hero and commander of the Alamo, Colonel William B. Travis. The line in the sand represents total commitment. Once crossed, there is no going back. It's not crossing this line – the lack of total commitment – that trips most new start-up business owners.

lip service, *n*. Fake excitement that you're on board with the vice president's enthusiastic, "We're going to turn this ship around and this will be our best year ever!" The VP doesn't know that you've seen her résumé and job search posted on the Internet.

list broker, *n*. Company that collects contact information on prospective buyers from magazines, newspapers, the Internet, and other sources to sell them to salespeople to find leads. Where your junk mail originates.

"Check us out for the most complete and up-to-date lists on everyone in America and the world!" – *NSA*

list price, *n*. What the seller would like you to pay. What you're not going to pay. What's negotiable.

listen, *v*. Men don't. Ask any woman. "Hey! What are you doing? What did I just tell you?"

"No one really listens to anyone else, and if you try it for a while, you'll see why." – *Mignon McLaughlin*

livery driver, *n*. Private car service drivers who hang around airports and are not allowed to solicit rides from arriving passengers; but they do it anyway by ripping the luggage from their hands in the terminal and racing them to their black Town Car parked curbside.

"If you're the designated driver, have fun with it. At the end of the night drop the people off at the wrong houses." – *Jeff Foxworthy*

lobbyist, *n*. They know people and they know how to game the system. What corrupt and unscrupulous politicians become once their voters have had enough and turn them out. Not to worry – they're just changing zip codes, not principles. They never worked for the voters anyway.

"We've already established what you are. Now we're just haggling over the price." – *Winston Churchill*

location, *n*. If repeated quickly three times, you're talking with a real estate agent.

115

logical, *adj*. Oooookay.
"You sound reasonable. Better up my medication." – *Unknown*

long shot, *n*. Early check-in at the hotel.

looky-loo, *n*. The guy in the electronics section pestering the salesperson with no intention of buying, while waiting for his wife to try on different outfits in the women's section. Spread the misery.

loophole, *n*. What attorneys are paid to hide in contracts hoping the opposing attorneys can't find them. The smaller the print the bigger the loophole. Most creative loopholes are put into the tax codes like Florida's "Rent-a-Cow" credit that gives a tax break to landowners who put a few cows on their property or lawns to be managed by rent-a-ranchers.

lose-lose, *adj*. Two pessimists negotiating.
"A pessimist is one who complains about the noise when opportunity knocks." – *Unknown*

loss, *n*. A lesson waiting to be learned.
"Life provides losses and heartbreak for all of us. But the greatest tragedy is to have the experience, and miss the meaning." – *Unknown*

loss leader, *n*. Legal, but barely a step above bait-and-switch.
"Grocery stores never put their bread and milk on the same side of the store. They want you to have to walk through the store to the other side knowing you'll stop and pick up something else." – *Uncle Togie, former Austin grocery store owner**

lost, *adj*. Like your keys, you're not lost – you just don't know where you are.
"We're lost, but we're making good time." – *Yogi Berra*

lowest bidder, *n*. Provider of an inferior product who throws in a moving religious experience, gratis. What you think about as you watch the plane's frozen wings flap up and down as it screams down the ice-covered concrete at 150 m.p.h. More prayers are said on takeoffs and landings each day than in every church in a year.

low-hanging fruit, *n*. Easy pickings – what all salespeople look for in a customer: a need, a want, and money. Desperation is the closer. Ticket scalpers outside a sold out game or concert are at the conflux of the perfect storm.

luck, *n*. Something you had nothing to do with, but you'll still take all the credit.
"The one thing we want. The one thing we need. The one thing we can't count on. Luck." – *Nick Heller*

lunch, *n*. A businessperson's watering hole where there is an unspoken truce among all predators gathered around.
"I was going to take you out to lunch for your birthday – but you already are." – *Unknown*

M

magic, *n.* Sleight of hand. How books are cooked.

"There is no such thing as magic. It's nothing but tricks and deceit." – *Penn Jillette of Penn and Teller*

magician, *n.* Book cooker.

major account, *n.* Like a rich, spoiled diva, they're high maintenance accounts that get away with bullying and threatening their vendors until they get their way. That, and they never pay on time.

"By the time (Alex Rodriguez) reached the Texas Rangers, a clubhouse attendant was required to put a dab of toothpaste on his toothbrush after every game. Of course, this sort of egomaniacal behavior alienated him from his team." – *David Brooks, New York Times*

management by walking around. Upper management trying to figure out what your job is, what you're doing, and why you're doing it that way.

manager, *n*. A company's broker who negotiates the corporate policies from above with those who must implement them below to achieve the different goals that each group wants. Juggling buzzing chainsaws would be less stressful and less dangerous.

"What do you need from management? What else can we do to help make you better and increase your sales?" – *Branch manager's entreaty to her sales team every day that led to her division leading all the corporation's other branches in sales every year**

mandatory attendance, *n*. No required meeting is ever going to end well.

mantra, *n*. Affirmations that create beliefs.

"I think I can. I think I can. I think I can." – *The Little Engine That Could*

manufacturer, *n*. Inadvertent producer of torts, litigation, and class action lawsuits. Their overseas sweat shops can even do it with child labor at a fraction of the cost.

manufacturer's rep, *n*. Salesman who gets to choose the products he wants to sell. Sweet!

MapQuest, *n*. Turn-by-turn directions for mobile devices that get you where you want to go using the most circuitous route, traversing through every hood in the city. Your vehicle may end up in a lake nowhere close to your chosen destination. Bring fishing poles, paddles, and life jackets. A rescue app is optional.

"I stumble around. That's what I do. And sometimes I stumble in the right direction." – *Inspector Morse*

margin of error, *n*. The flexibility you feel you have when driving over the speed limit before being pulled over.

market, *v.* To showcase and advertise goods and services in glitzy, revealing, and tantalizing ways in hopes of finding buyers. Police call it prostitution.

"The superior man understands what is right; the inferior man understands what will sell." – *Confucius*

marketing, *v.* The seductress of sales. The smell of grilled onions and burgers coming through the deliciously smoky haze on the fair's midway.

markup, *n.* The selling price generating a profit on a product, created on the fly by adding an amount pulled out of thin air to the cost of the product. "How much?" the RV buyer asks. "How much do you want to spend?" responds the salesman.

mayhem, *n.* Trying to get to any Los Angeles area airport on the freeways on a winter's dark, late Friday afternoon in the rain. Mayhem descends into panic as you search in vain to find a service station near the airport to top off your rental car's tank so you won't be ripped off by the agency for returning it only three-quarters full. And, oh yeah, your plane boards in forty minutes.

mediate, *v.* To bring two adversaries together to compromise on a solution that will end the bickering. "Billy! You and your sister get in here this minute! We're going to put an end to this nonsense!" Neither party is satisfied with the outcome, but they live in fear the mediator will find even more unappealing solutions.

meditate, *v.* What you're doing at your desk when your boss finds you snoring.

"Out of body. Back in twenty minutes." – *Sign on the door of a meditation center*

meeting, *n*. Please, God! Not another one!

"I have noticed that the people who are late to meetings are often so much jollier than the people who have to wait for them." – *E.V. Lucas*

memorize, *v.t.* To steal with the mind.

"If I ever lose my cell phone, I've got no idea what my friends phone numbers are. I've never had a need to learn them." – *College student*

mentor, *n*. Someone who has answers for those wanting to ask the questions. It's like a fishing guide who knows how deep the fish are, what they're biting, and how to rig the line; but you've got to want to do the work to catch the fish.

"I was always glad to help any of the players if they asked for my help. But if they didn't, I never volunteered it because they weren't ready to listen." – *Steve Largent, Seattle Seahawks Hall of Famer*

merger, *n*. The end of your job as you know it.

metaphor, *n*. A direct comparison between things often with one word used symbolically to represent another. "Sales support is the nanny of prima donnas."

métier, *n*. One's area of expertise and calling. "He knew he was destined to be in sales when he saw his competition."

"What would I do if the principal told me to call back after five? I wouldn't. I get off at five. My day is done." – *Cincinnati salesman's response to the seminar speaker's question, to which a lady in the back yelled, "Give me his number. I'll call him!"**

micromanagement, *n*. Backseat driver style of management.

micromanager, *n*. Mom.

"'Let me smell that shirt,' mom demanded. 'Yeah. That's good for another week.'" – *Unknown*

middle manager, *n*. Akin to a sewage pipe: has to take crap coming from those managed below, as well as crap from the bosses above, with no outlet to expel the waste. It stinks.

"Being a manager is simple. All you have to do is to keep the five players who hate your guts away from the five who are undecided." – *Casey Stengel*

mingle, *v*. Meeting and mixing with like-minded individuals with common interests. It's like 65,000 rabid football fans cheering the team on, except with fewer rabid people, no football team, and no cheerleaders.

minimum wage, *n*. This week's groceries. What the rich think is too much.

"The current federal minimum wage is $7.25 an hour and Congress doesn't want to raise it. At the same time the salary for Congress comes in at $70 an hour. I think it's ridiculous that Congress is even getting paid because they're not doing their job." – *The Cycle*

mirror technique, *n*. Subtle, subconscious technique of influence when you copy the words and mannerisms of the other person so they think they're looking into the mirror at their most favorite person in the world. If it looks like a duck, walks like a duck, and quacks like a duck, then so do you.

"You mirror people every day. When talking to a child, don't you drop down to their level and use words they understand? Watching the game on the big screen with your friends, don't you talk, laugh, and horse around like they do? When you have a big meeting with important clients, don't you dress, talk, and act to look like them?" – *Response to business owner who said she would never mirror someone as it's too manipulative*

mission creep, *n*. An organization's singular objective that gradually broadened to add more objectives. Amazon started as a bookseller, but now sells more products than any retailer. Nordstrom started as a shoe merchant and grew into a purveyor of classy fashions for all. It's like an innocent date that turned into romance that turned into marriage that turned into kids that turned into excruciating holidays with in-laws.

"Come here you little creep!" – *Uncle to nephew who just doused him with a water balloon at the July 4th family reunion*

mission statement, *n*. A company's business purpose that no one believes.

"It may be that your sole purpose in life is simply to serve as a warning to others." – *Unknown*

misspoke, *v*. The truth slipped out and now you have to say you didn't mean it although you still believe it.

mistakes, *n.pl*. Teachers we try to avoid and eliminate. The more you make, the more you learn. Some are costly, most are just embarrassing. Cousins to problems and failures.

"When anyone in our family makes a mistake, we admit it. That's why so many of us are in jail." – *The Middle*

misunderstanding, *n*. You just don't get it.

"It depends upon what *is* is." – *Bill Clinton*

misunderstood, *n*. When someone says "you misunderstood what I said", you didn't.

"I have suffered from being misunderstood, but I would have suffered a hell of a lot more if I had been understood." – *Clarence Darrow*

The Wickedly Fun Dictionary of Business

MLM, *n*. Multi-Level Marketing. It's like being a salesperson with no sales skills, a sales recruiter with no recruiting background, a sales trainer with no teaching skills, a manager who's never managed, and practicing psychology after reading one of Dr. Phil's books. What could possibly go wrong?

"If a friend tells you she has a great opportunity she'd like to show you, but won't tell you what it is unless she can come to your home, you can take it to the bank that it's a multi-level marketing deal." – *Wary Indianapolis businesswoman**

mojo, *n*. A magic spell that may be required to get into that chic Washington D.C. restaurant you failed to make reservations for before you left town. "Have you met President Mojo?" you ask the maître d' as you palm him a crisp new $100 bill. You'll probably be snubbed and lose the presidency at the same time, but it's worth the try.

Monday, *n*. The most unpopular day of the week, which is why so few show up.

"It's amusing to see who doesn't show up for work when the weather is bad. It's usually the people we could do without any day." – *Andy Rooney*

money, *n*. Fickled. The root of all evil. The answer to your prayers. Wall Street's fertilizer. The seed of greed. Politician's palm grease.

"You have reached the pinnacle of success as soon as you become uninterested in money, compliments, or publicity." – *Thomas Wolfe*

money laundering. Removing criminal fingerprints from dirty money washed through Super PAC laundromats sanctioned by the Supreme Court in *Citizens United v. Federal Election Committee.*

monologue, *n*. A one-way conversation with your boss where you're the audience. Standing ovation appreciated.

monopoly, *n.* The power to deal from the bottom of the deck and no one can call you on it.

moonlight, *v.i.* A second job to try to make ends meet. Not nearly as glamorous as it sounds. It's the nightlight for migrant farm workers, many of whom live and sleep in their cars in the fields as they travel from farm to farm to pick the crops.

moonshot idea. It's that idea you had, but didn't act on because you thought it was silly – only to find someone else took the idea a year later and is now making millions. Also, an idea that causes you to slap yourself on the head and moan, "Why didn't I think of that?"
"It's not a bad idea until you've tried it." – *Lie to Me*

moot, *adj.* A salesperson's plea to management to get telemarketers to make cold calls for him, because his time is "too valuable".
"It's easy to find people who can sell. But I hire salespeople who know how to find the people to sell to. If you can't cold call, you can't sell for me." – *Craig McCaw, billionaire cell phone pioneer**

moron, *n.* Anyone not you.
"I am amazed at radio DJs today. I am firmly convinced that AM on my radio stands for Absolute Moron. I will not begin to tell you what FM stands for." – *Jasper Carrott*

motivate, *v.t.* A cattle prod that moves the cows to where they don't want to go. Yee-haw!
"I just wake up and say, 'You're a bum – go do something worthwhile today.'" – *Garth Brooks*

motivation, *n.* Anything that will compel the body to go from being a body at rest to being a body in motion. Point to the floor and scream, "Snake!" Guaranteed to work with groups or individuals 100% of the time.

"Motivation is the car's ignition." – *Zig Ziglar*

mouth, *n*. Too often speaks before the brain is through downloading.

"Stereotypes are often more about feelings than facts. Which makes them a lot like women." – *Cal FitzSimmons*

moxie, *n*. It's either brassiness or lunacy. For example, any guy not an Olympic swimmer wearing Speedos.

MSRP, *n*. Manufacturer's Suggested Retail Price. It's your doctor bill before the insurance payment and doctor's write-off.

multitask, *v.i.* Doing three things at once: driving, texting, and wrecking.

"We saw the teenage driver texting with both hands while steering with her foot!" – *Shocked mom**

my bad, *n*. Making light of the fact that it's your fault, even though it's a major screw up, and hoping people won't be too hard on you. Like the NASCAR driver apologizing for a twenty car pileup. "My bad!"

my call, *n*. The call the prospect won't take or return. Also, taking responsibility for your decision. If it turns out to be a bad decision, grab some clothes pins because you're going to be hung out to dry.

MYOB. Mind Your Own Business. The motto Ben Franklin wanted for U.S. currency. Mission statement for spy services. Sign on your teen's bedroom door.

mystery, *n*. Why can't you do what you know how to do when it needs to be done?

mystery shopper, *n.* Shoplifter.

N

nailed it. Go-o-o-o-o-o-o-al!!!

names, *n.pl.* Nouns on the tip of the tongue that don't match the faces. A memory test easily failed. A phone book without them is just a book of numbers.

"One of the highest rated talents you can have in business is the ability to remember names. And one of the most damaging attributes that causes more lost sales is the inability to remember names." – *Harry Lorayne, memory expert*

"The number one memory complaint people have is that they're bad with names." – *Majid Fotuhi, M.D., neurologist*

nanny, *n.* Parent outsourcing.

napkin technique, *n.* Send a napkin to your prospect and write on it, "The best deals are done on the back of a napkin. Have lunch with me and I'll prove it."

"Wild horses couldn't drag a secret out of most women over lunch. However, women seldom have lunch with wild horses." – *Ivern Boyett*

narcissism, *n*. Enough about you, let's talk about me. Narcissists can't tear themselves away from themselves, not that they'd try. Easy to start and carry on conversations with them: "So, tell me about yourself." If there should be a lull, "Got any pictures of yourself?"

"There is only one beautiful child in the world, and my mother has it." – *Unknown*

narcissist, *n*. He easily implodes by being a politician, with a camera, while on Twitter.

"Think about it. Should New York really have a mayor called 'Carlos Danger'?" – *David Letterman on failed mayoral candidate Anthony Weiner's nom de guerre*

need, *n*. Need is a necessity like air, water, food. Want is a desire for anything else: a car, a boat, a vacation. Sales is about turning wants into needs.

"I don't need you anymore – and I don't want you." – *Damages's attorney Patty Hewes to estranged husband Phil*

need to know. A nicer way to say "butt out".

needs analysis, *n*. Sales survey to convert wants into needs. "You need some tax write-offs. So what you want is a 414-foot megayacht to entertain your clients. You'll have helicopter pads fore and aft, which leaves plenty of room for the seven tenders, including a 63-foot one docked on the transom, a swimming pool aft on one of the upper decks, and side hatches at the water line to serve as a dock for your jet skis. Of course, you'll have your two submarines included as well." (Actual description of Microsoft co-founder Paul Allen's *Octopus* superyacht.)

"For every 30 days it's here, it will spend roughly $2.7 million on repairs and services – roughly $90,000 a day." – *Seattle Times report on the larger 440-foot superyacht Serene docked in Elliott Bay and owned by Russian vodka distributor Yuri Scheffler*

negotiate, *v.* Bargaining when one party either doesn't believe it's a fair deal, or when he wants something he doesn't deserve. Like hostage takers in a bank heist trying to work out a deal for a plane and free ride to the airport.

"Your strength in negotiations is when you can say, 'Okay, let's not do it.'" – *Louis C.K.*

nerd, *n.* The geek's boss. The richest man in the building.

"I didn't understand a thing he was talking about." – *Flummoxed executive leaving a tech seminar*

net price, *n.* Take away the discounts and rebates and you have what's coming out of your wallet. Smart buyers start negotiating at the net. After the price is agreed upon, they'll throw in their coupons, thus creating an unexpected net-net price for the surprised seller.

network marketing, *n.* Multi-level marketing: Mary Kay, Avon, Herbalife, Pampered Chef. Includes some religious groups who park their cars down the street and try to sneak up on you with their pamphlets.

networking, *n.* What's done to avoid cold calling, yet 90% of networkers are uncomfortable in walking over and introducing themselves to strangers (a cold call) at a networking function. Networkers trade names of unsuspecting marks to get leads. The irony is the leads are never called because they require – you guessed it – a cold call.

"There are two kinds of people in the world: those who come into a room and say, 'Here I am!' and those who come in and say, 'Oh, there you are.'" – *Unknown*

new and improved, *n.* Your second child.

"Thank goodness he's nothing like his older brother." – *Many moms*

nibble, *v*. Trial close. "Let's throw this figure out and see if we get a nibble." If no nibble, change the bait.

niche marketing, *n*. An isolated market of clients a salesperson specializes in. For sales reps of B2 Stealth bombers, they have only one.

nickel-and-diming, *v.t*. Scurrilous negotiating technique when the other party asks for a concession without wanting to give one in return, using the innocent phrase, "Oh, by the way, would you mind throwing in...?" To stop this from happening, ask for something in return. "Maybe. I'll take it back to the boss to get her approval. But if she gives it, she'll want something in return. And what she wants is an introduction to three buyers you network with. Deal?" They'll think twice before trying this again.

nightmare, *n*. What happens when the vendor with the lowest bid wins the contract, when he was just clowning around to see if he could throw a monkey wrench into the normally rigged bidding procedures.

"He is simply a shiver looking for a spine to run up." – *Paul Keating*

no, *adv*. Final decision not in your favor. It doesn't mean, "Maybe. Why don't you try again?"

"How can I say 'No' to you – and yet I have." – *Nora Ephron*

no comment, *n*. Good legal advice when caught red-handed. Wrong response to spouse or partner who catches you.

no compete contract, *n*. A condition of employment at some companies. This is the company's assurance that if there is a later mutiny, the employee will not pirate and plunder their customer base. Aargh!

no disrespect, *n.* A pre-apology before the affront commences.

"I have too much respect for the truth to drag it out on every trifling occasion." – *Mark Twain*

no solicitors, *n.* Sign on office doors warning salespeople not to enter or suffer the consequences. The last thing you remember seeing when waking up in the emergency room.

no win, *n.* No matter what you say or do, there's no way you're getting out of the predicament you've gotten yourself into. It's agreeing to be the bridesmaid before you've seen the dress.

"Life is not a spectacle or a feast; it is a predicament." – *George Santayana*

nonprofit, *n.* Many worthy charities and organizations use this status to give them more resources to help others. But too many use this tax shield to buffalo vendors into giving them a deeper discount; yet they pay exorbitant salaries to executives while holding annual meetings at exotic locales. The NFL is a nonprofit organization even though it makes over $9 billion a year in *profits*, spends over $1.1 million a year in lobbying, makes about $250 million each year on the Super Bowl, and pays its commissioner a $20-$30 million annual salary. With other leagues like the NFL and PGA using the nonprofit status, taxpayers subsidize them to the tune of over $90 million a year.

"I guess when we get requests for proposals from companies that stress they're nonprofits, they expect us to not make a profit either?" – *Charlotte, North Carolina printer saleswoman*

not interested, *n.* Knee-jerk response to a cold caller's opening statement. Indication that changes need to be made.

not my job. If your boss hears you say this, you'll be right.

notes, *n.pl.* If there should be discrepancies between what the customer says and what the salesperson hears, the one with the best notes wins. It shows the customer you're listening and that what he has to say is important. The person who takes notes will increase their retention by over 25%, and be more likely to take action on what they write down.

"Why aren't you taking notes? This is important! You're not going to remember it. I'm expecting you to follow-up." – *Disgruntled customer to salesperson who he's called onto the carpet to voice his complaints**

nuance, *n.* A subtle difference often missed by one and enthusiastically pointed out by the other who sees it.

"You're *other* left, dummy!" – *Air Force training instructor yelling at raw recruit who did a right-face when told to do a left-face**

number two, *n.* The best position to be in with the prospect if you're not number one, because when things change – and they will – they're only calling number two. Or, that's what your infant just did.

numbers game, *n.* The myth that if you make "X" number of calls you'll make "Y" number of sales, without taking into account the salesperson's passion, skills, and perseverance to get the job done. It's like telling you to stand on the mound at Yankee stadium, giving you a ball, and promising that if you make enough pitches you'll be an All-Star.

O

objection, *n*. Nit-picking complaint to avoid making a decision or to accept the inevitable. It's what your father-in-law tried to raise at the wedding but was shushed.

"The best way to deal with an objection is to bring it up first. Price is always an objection. Bring it up before you even do the presentation. 'Before I show you the unit you're interested in, I must warn you that it is among the most expensive on the market. But we have similar units that are a little *cheaper*. Would you rather see them instead?'" – *Sony regional sales manager who also suggested throwing in there are "cheaper" alternatives, because the customer will then try to prove that he can afford the more expensive one**

objective, *n*. What people fail to identify before starting the work. What you need to know so you'll know what you need to do to get it. Not knowing your objective is like taking a paintball gun to hunt grizzlies.

"The end is where we start from." – *T.S. Eliot*

obstacles, *n.pl*. What you see when you don't want to do what needs to be done.

"It's cold. It's hot. It's rainy. It's snowy. It's Monday. It's Friday. It's early. It's late." – *Salespeople's excuses for not cold calling**

offer, *v*. When negotiating parties test each other to see if the other has done their homework, and if they have the conviction to ask for what they feel they deserve.

office park, *n*. Prospecting obstacle course for outside salespeople. Where cold callers feel like animals in a zoo because everyone is peering at them from behind the glass windows from surrounding offices, watching their every move. Zoos have "Do Not Feed the Animals" warnings. Office parks have their "No Solicitors!" warnings.

off-the-books, *adj*. Political junkets, tip jars, and your kids' allowances. American gray underground economy where more than $2 trillion went unreported to the I.R.S. in 2012 (*The New Yorker*).

"We'll always be best friends – because you know too much." – *Unknown*

off-the-record, *adj*. Cross your heart and hope to die if you tell anyone I said this. If you tell them, I'll deny I said it and call you a liar. She said/she said deniability.

"She said she would deny it and she's denying it." – *Hoboken, New Jersey, Mayor Dawn Zimmer to CNN about Lt. Governor Kim Guadagno who Zimmer said was trying to muscle her into approving a development project in her city before hurricane Sandy relief funds would be released (January 21, 2014)*

old boys' network, *n*. A mysterious, protective clique of wealthy and influential businessmen with secret handshakes and covert rituals. It's like dealing with the Federal Reserve or the all-male Catholic hierarchy of Popes, cardinals, bishops, and patriarchs. God help us!

on the fly. Making it up as you go. Creative ideas triggered by desperate situations.

"The airline cancelled my connecting flight from San Francisco to Sacramento, so I hitched a ride with some other stranded passengers who rented a car." – *Saleswoman who had to be in Sacramento that day**

open door policy, *n*. How SWAT teams announce their arrival.

open-ended, *adj*. A questioning technique that allows spontaneous and unguided responses in hopes of trapping the responder in her own words. Technique used by detectives when asking questions like, "What do you know about the circus elephant's missing trunk?" It's as good as giving someone a shovel and letting them dig their own grave.

opening statement, *n*. Start at the end.

"New speakers save their best for last and put it in the conclusion. By then the audience's attention has wandered. Instead, move your conclusion to the opening statement since that's what you want the people to remember." – *Toastmasters**

opinion, *n*. A belief in search of believers.

"The best advice I can give is to ignore advice. Life is too short to be distracted by the opinions of others." – *Russel Edson*

OPM, *n.* Other People's Money. Pickpocket investing. It's when you don't believe enough in your idea to bet the house on it and cajole others to bet theirs. Either that or you're starting a Ponzi scheme.

opportunity, *n.* Usually not. "Have I got an opportunity for you!" Best understood as a question, and not as a fact.

optimist, *n.* Children before they hit middle school. Someone who can still smile at the dentist with a rubber dam in her mouth. Often confused with optometrist.

"Being an optimist after you've got everything you want doesn't count." – *Kin Hubbard*

opt-in, *v.i.* The high school brainiac in calculus always raising her hand because she has the answers.

"I've only given two 'D's' in twenty years of teaching. You either pass or fail. The 'D' is for a student who gives his best – really tries – but just doesn't 'get it'." – *Recipient of one of the two D's**

opt-out, *v.i.* Ducking your head and averting your eyes when volunteers are sought for the PTSA fundraiser.

order takers, *n.pl.* What management considers 80% of their sales team to be.

ordinary things, *n.* The basics. Easy-to-do things that, if you do them, will make you better and impress others: remembering names, being on time, doing your homework, asking better questions, listening, avoiding interruptions.

"How well do you do the ordinary things?" – *Question drilled into the heads of his players by former major league baseball manager Lou Pinella*

organizational chart, *n*. A maze of boxes with names and lines showing importance in the organization and who reports to whom. It's safe to assume that the higher up the chart, the more predatory the chart climber. That's why each box has a head-shot silhouette of the box holder looking over their shoulder.

outside salesperson, *n*. A company's sales detective always looking for clues to increase their sales, going door-to-door looking for suspects, working their contacts, following up on all leads, and trying to close more deals. The best ones have the same attitude as police detectives: "Will this work? I don't know. Let's try it and see what happens."

outsourcing, *v.t.* Jobs exporting. Remember when mom told you to "eat all your peas" and to "think of all those poor people in third world countries who can't afford peas"? No longer a worry. Now they have your job – and you can no longer afford peas.

overstocked, *n*. A pretext company's use to get rid of excess inventory that won't sell: "We're overstocked! Again! Everything must go!" Why not fire the person who keeps ordering the wrong stock instead?

own it. "It's your baby!" What the doctor says in the delivery room.

owner, *n*. When you can no longer sleep through the night.

ownership, *n*. To take responsibility for your work. But unlike the boss's ownership, you don't share in the bonuses, profits, or equity – only the losses.

P

pact, *n*. A pinkie-promise between salespeople not to invade the others' territories (unless there is an account in there they really, really want). Much like the Great White Father's treaties with the Native Americans.

pains me to say. Spoken by someone who isn't – and won't be – in the same amount of pain as the listener is about to be. "It pains me to say that because we didn't meet our team sales projection, not everyone will be getting a bonus this quarter." The phrase "not everyone" is the scalpel that cuts out the speaker's pain.

palm down handshake, *n*. Easiest way to identify top-level decision makers since 78% use this put-down greeting to get the upperhand. Most Driver personalities use this handshake as well. That's why it's entertaining to watch two Drivers trying to greet each other. The message is clear: "I want to be in control; I give the orders; you obey." Used by either sex on either sex.

"A tactic perceived is no longer a tactic." – *General George S. Patton*

palm up handshake, *n.* The magic handshake to gain immediate trust, build rapport, and get the other party to spill their secrets. The palm up tells the other person you're willing to "give them the floor", to listen to what they have to say. They trust you and like you, but don't know why. The best handshake to use in business. Since you *initiated* the palm up handshake, the palm down handshake rules don't apply.

"My daughter and I visited four car dealerships as she was car shopping. I asked which of the four salesmen she liked best. (I had written '3' on a slip of paper without showing her.) 'I liked the third one, but don't know why.' I showed her the paper. 'How did you know?' He was the only one to use the palm up handshake. The other three salesmen used the palm down handshake." – *Jerry Hocutt*

paperwork, *n.* A good excuse. "Hey, wanna do lunch?" Sorry. Too much paperwork.

paradigm, *n.* When your boss points you out to the rest of the staff as someone *not* to emulate, you've just become an unwitting paradigm.

paradox of cold calling, *n.* Strange but true: if you try to be a coward when cold calling (hyperventilate, become nervous, have your mind go blank) the exact opposite will occur – you calm down immediately, become focused, and gather courage. The same concept applies when interviewing for a job. Paradoxical intention: try to make something you don't want to happen, happen, and the opposite happens. The mind is a strange place to be in.

"I knew I'd fail the test. I just didn't 'get' the material. So I didn't study the week before. I gave up. I told myself, 'I'll show my professor how really stupid I am. I'll just screw it all up.' I ended up making an A. The answers just came to me." – *College student telling how paradoxical intention helped her to ace an exam**

paranoia, *n*. It's the new management team that you're sure is out to get you. And that's what they want you to think. Crazy, huh!

"If you would know who controls you, see who you may not criticize." – *Tacitus*

Pareto principle, *n*. The 80/20 rule: 80% of the sales are made by 20% of the salespeople. The principle expanded: sales managers are looking to replace 80% of the sales team 100% of the time.

partner, *n*. In business, your equal. At home, your superior.

part-time jobs, *n. pl.* What social media and the Internet have turned full-time jobs into.

passion, *n*. What will get you hired when you don't have the experience. Passion allows you to be embarrassed, to be vulnerable, to do the work without any guarantees of success. It allows you to be you with no pretensions.

"The first thing I look for in hiring any new salesperson is their passion. I can teach them every sales skill. But I can't teach them passion." – *Canadian sales manager for international company**

passive-aggressive, *adj*. Social media; email; texting. Unassertive, negative aggression you're afraid to say face-to-face. Threat made indirectly like, "Did I see you calling on accounts in my territory?" instead of naked aggression, "If I catch you in my territory again your voice is going to be three octaves higher buster!"

"If they can put a man on the moon, why can't they put them all there?" – *Jill (graffiti on a bathroom wall)*

password, *n*. What hackers can find on your computer but you can't.

patience, *n.* Waiting for the trap to spring. "Let's give her the option and see what she does."

"In an ambush situation, waiting is what wins the battle. You need infinite patience. No use fretting or worrying. You just wait. Doing nothing, thinking nothing, burning no energy. Waiting is a skill like anything else." – *Lee Child*

patronize, *v.t.* Used smartly, it's a good way to challenge someone to get the job done.

"I don't know if this is something your company can do, and if not, maybe you can refer me to your competitor, but...." – *Statement used to get emergency printing done overnight for workbooks by speaker on the road; response was always, "Of course we can"**

pause, *n.* Calculated silence. What speakers should do to let the listener digest what was said, and to catch up on the idea presented. A pause puts emphasis on what was said – a silent exclamation point.

pay phones, *n.pl.* Like the telegraph and rotary phones, it's something you'll have a hard time explaining to your grandkids some day.

payback, *n.* Karma's due.

penny for your thoughts. You either have worthless ideas, or you're dealing with the CFO.

"Our best friends and our worst enemies are our thoughts. A thought can do us more good than a doctor or a banker or a faithful friend. It can also do us more harm than a brick." –*Frank Crane*

people skills, *n.pl.* The ability to connect, to relate. Bedside manners. Your favorite aunt.

"Show up in other people's lives." – *Sargent Shriver*

Pepsi technique, *n*. If possible, buy and use your prospect's product to land the appointment.

"I got the appointment and landed the Pepsi account in New York by sending the buyer an empty Pepsi bottle with this note: 'I tried your product, will you try mine?'" – *Long Island saleswoman**

perceive, *v.t.* To intuitively become aware of what's about to happen. For example, when the desk clerk says, "We're all booked and can't seem to find a record of your reservation," it pretty much tells you that you won't be spending the night where you thought.

perfect, *n*. Works for me. "Part of our job interview requires a polygraph exam, but the equipment is broken, so we'll just have to take your word for it." Perfect.

"Being the best doesn't mean being perfect." – *Bones*

perfection, *n*. What we seek, never expecting to find.

"Have no fear of perfection – you'll never reach it." – *Salvador Dali*

performance bonus, *n*. It's like an executive tip jar where they feel like the millions they're paid to do their job isn't enough, and more is needed so they can furnish their fourth home in the Hamptons.

"Performance bonuses for many of the CEO's is an oxymoron. I would tell them, (a) you don't deserve a bonus, (b) (on their threat to quit and go elsewhere) where are you going to go? and (c) if you want to go, go." – *Andrew Cuomo*

performance review, *n*. Confirmation of what you suspected.

"The employee is depriving a village somewhere of an idiot." – *Comment on employee's review*

perk, *n.* For executives, it's exclusive athletic club memberships. For the staff, it's Wednesday Yoga classes in the basement (after-hours, of course). It's Hot Yoga if the basement has no windows. And it's Hot Stinky Yoga if the basement has no windows and ventilation.

permission, *n.* Approval sought by those who are indecisive, don't know if it's the right thing to do, and don't want the responsibility.

permission marketing, *n.* Customers' implied consent to be approached by salespeople when entering the store. "Just looking" expresses consent has been revoked.

persistent, *adj.* Borderline stalkers. Won't give up; keeps trying; not discouraged; strong willed; searching for another angle.
"If you ever leave me, I'll go with you." – *Rene Taylor*

personalities, *n.pl.* Basically four types (see *Analytical, Driver, Expressive, Amiable personalities*). If you can learn to read them, it's as close to mind reading as you'll get. You'll know how long they take to make decisions, how much information to give them, if they want to do all the talking, if they like small talk, and even how they'll try to impress you. For example, if you read just the first line in this definition and moved on to the next definition – you're a Driver. Too many words, too much detail. (And you're not even reading this far to see that you're being made fun of.) If you're still reading this, you're an Analytical. You need more words, more explanations, more detail. But I'm not giving them to you. I'm going now. Don't follow.

personalize, *v.t.* An exclusive touch to make something more special and meaningful. Like an autographed book; or your own court docket number for the ticket you're contesting for being pulled over while talking on your cell phone.

perspective, *n*. Your view to try and persuade the other side that he didn't see what he thought he saw. The coach's red flag challenge to the referee's TD call. The manager kicking dirt on the home plate after the umpire's called out. The saleswoman pointing out the flaws of the customer's decision to go with the competition.

"President to competitor's general manager: 'Your salesman told my prospect you have ten times more transmitters and better coverage in western Washington than we do, and I'm mad.' General manager: 'Isn't it true?' President: 'Yes, but he shouldn't be telling them that.'" – *General manager telling me of the conversation, laughing, and congratulating me on the sale**

persuade, *v.t.* To have a better story than the person you need to convince.

"I sit here all day trying to persuade people to do the things they ought to have sense enough to do without my persuading them. That's all the powers of the president amount to." – *Harry S. Truman*

pessimist, *n*. The brake on the optimist's car.

"No sense being pessimistic. It wouldn't work anyway." – *Unknown*

pest, *n*. A nag you can't ride or shoot. The service department's nemesis: a customer who won't read the instructions and can't follow directions.

petty cash, *n*. The funding source for your raise.

philanthropist, *n*. What you become when you have so much money you can't leave any more to the kids.

phishing, *n*. An email scam to steal confidential information from the recipient to use illegally. In school, it was that kid behind you in class who was always trying to look over your shoulder to steal your test answers. At work, it's the co-worker who steals your idea and takes it to the boss as his.

phone booth, *n*. They had to be discontinued because too many confused them with Porta-Potties.

phone it in. A job applicant who shows up for the interview unprepared. A retiree's last days on the job. The salesperson who met her quota early and coasts the rest of the month. The professional pitcher with a 7-0 lead in the fourth who loses his focus and then the game.

phony, *n*. The faces we wear to influence others to believe what we want them to believe: a clown's face, the game face, our "work" face.
    "Drop the act. I'm on to you." – *Mom to teen's sad face**

pick your brains. Done over lunch. In nature, it's vultures feeding on roadkill. In business, how people butter up experts to get free information. In both cases, once the brain has been picked clean, no thank you notes are left behind. Bur-r-r-r-p!
    "People call me all the time and ask to buy me lunch so they can 'pick my brain.' My response is, 'I have a $500 per hour brain-picking fee and I'll buy your lunch.' That stops all the bloodsuckers, and I make about $5,000 a year eating lunch." – *Jeffrey Gitomer*

pick-up line, *n*. A cold caller's opening line that was accidentally originated in bars by an auto parts salesman from Pittsburgh in 1935: "Hey! Wanna see my lug nuts?"

pink slips, *n.pl*. Something found on employees' desks after the hostile takeover – and it's not something sheer and frilly from Victoria's Secret.

pitch, *v.* Sales spiel. Don't be coy. Be direct and cut to the chase.

"A hint is the hardest kind of request to decode and the easiest to refuse." – *Malcolm Gladwell*

planted information, *n.* Corporate espionage and chicanery. False information leaked to gain the advantage. If written, deemed to be the "real thing" even though it's not. Most effective if discovered and not left out in the open.

plausible, *adj.* Possibly believable, but not likely. "Let's run it up the flagpole and see who salutes."

plausible deniability. Keep it to yourself. Don't tell me. It's refusing to see or seek the truth in order to maintain innocence, especially if jail time is possible. It's the ostrich with its head in the ground refusing to see the jackals salivating nearby.

"I had nothing to do with this: no knowledge, no authorization; no planning." – *New Jersey "hands-on" Governor Chris Christie saying he was unaware of Bridgegate (the George Washington Bridge lane closures on the busiest bridge in the world) until it was over; further, he didn't even hear about it on national TV and radio stations while it was happening over a four day period (Time, February 3, 2014)*

"I know – NOTHING!" – *Sgt. Hans Schultz, Hogan's Heroes*

play dumb, *v.i.* A confounding negotiating tactic where one party plays like she doesn't understand, thereby making the other party have to speak in clearer terms, spell out exact facts and figures, and overall destroying the other party's tactic to win by confusion. Damn!

"I'm not offended by all the dumb blond jokes because I know I'm not dumb – and I also know that I'm not blonde." – *Dolly Parton*

play it by ear. Improvisation. "Let's see if this works." Make sure these aren't your last words.

player, *n*. Someone with skin in the game and directly responsible for the final outcome. Players are actors in real time. They're not strategists. They're not critics. They're catalysts that make things happen. The quarterback, not the coach. The golfer, not the caddie. The worker, not the manager.

"The last-place finisher in an Omaha, Nebraska, fantasy football league has to get a tattoo – as chosen by the league champion. Say Roddy White drops a pass? That could be the difference between having a Bieber tattoo on your leg, or your thigh as normal as the day you were born." – *ESPN*

please hold, *v.t*. The inspiration for Edward Munch's *The Scream*. "Your call is important to us and will be answered in the order it was received. Please hold." "We'll be with you shortly. Please hold." "Thanks for your patience. Please hold." After thirty minutes of warbling elevator music: click, mmmmmmm. "You've been disconnected. Please call back. Your call is important to us."

poach, *v.t*. Time honored tradition of stealing the competitors' customers. "Fried" is when they steal yours.

poem, *n*. Short stories – really short! Models for writing: you learn how to say much with fewer words in more creative ways.

"Last night I held a lovely hand / It was so small and neat / I thought my heart with joy would burst / So wild was every beat. / No other hand unto my heart / Could greater pleasure bring / Than the one so dear I held last night. / Four Aces and a King" – *A Lovely Hand, Anonymous*

poetry, *n*. Rhyming tweets.

point man, *n*. Taking the lead; drawing the fire; courage to go into the unknown. Better to volunteer someone you don't like. "Nikki, why don't you take the point on this?" Short life expectancy.

poise, *n*. Cool under pressure; ability to think on your feet. It's smiling and pretending you're listening while trying to recall the name of the person speaking with you so you can introduce her to your associate.

"The wonderful thing about meeting strangers is that you never know if the next one is going to have a profound impact on the rest of your life." – *Benjamin Levy*

policy, *n*. Bureaucracy's excuse for not changing.

"One of the things about leadership is that you cannot be a moderate, balanced, thoughtful, careful articulator of policy. You've got to be on the lunatic fringe." – *Jack Welch*

political games, *n.pl*. Gamers doing and saying anything for their own survival and advancement, even though they know that what they're doing may not be right or moral. How politicians get elected and get committee chairs when they're morally corrupt and mentally bankrupt.

"I like political jokes unless they get elected." – *Unknown*

politically correct, *n*. To act and speak correctly so as to not offend anyone – dumbass.

politicians, *n.pl*. Bureaucratic salespeople who will sell anyone down the river if it's to their benefit. Give salespeople a bad name.

"That lowdown scoundrel deserves to be kicked to death by a jackass, and I'm just the one to do it." – *Texas congressional candidate*

politician's handshake, *n.* The "double" handshake where the other person encloses your right hand with both of their hands. Used to convey a feeling of sincerity, warmth, and trust. Problem is, the person on the receiving end immediately becomes suspicious. "What are you up to? What do you want? I better watch my wallet." They don't call it the politician's handshake for nothing.

Ponzi scheme, *n.* A trip to the cleaners. First clue you're getting taken is revealed in the politician's handshake. Modeled on federal government money management.

POS, *n.* Point of Sale. The checkout counter where friends tell you not to forget your breath mints.

positioning, *v.t.* It's the restaurant putting their smiling, attractive couples and parties by the front windows to draw in the crowds, and putting the single, lonely road warrior next to the swinging kitchen doors in the back.

"That is the thankless position of the father in the family: the provider for all, and the enemy of all." – *August Strindberg*

possible, *adj.* Not probable, but maybe. "Is it possible to get a raise?" Okay, probably not.

post office, *n.* Model for how to ignore customers wanting to give you money. A place where there is a counter for five clerks but only one is on duty while the other four are on break.

"When it's slow, we'll usually take a nap in one of the trailers on the back lot." – *Postal employee who works loading and unloading mail at a bulk mail center in Texas**

postal clerk, *n.* Where?!!

pound of flesh, *n.* What merchant Shylock wanted in Shakespeare's *Merchant of Venice* as security. Occurs in a negotiation when you've given everything you can give, and have nothing left to give but your first born. Which, on second thought, might not be such a bad deal after all.

power, *n*. Having it doesn't give you the ability to make good decisions; just to enforce the bad decisions you make.

"Power is like being a lady; if you have to say you are, you aren't." – *Margaret Thatcher*

power suit, *n*. Your best dress where all the bigwigs will be present. How you dress will change your attitude as well as the perception others have of you.

"Would you get on an airplane with two pilots who are wearing cut-off jeans?" – *Paul Fussell*

PowerPoint presentation, *n*. Stop it!

"When Jeff holds meetings at Amazon, he asks people not to use PowerPoints but to write an essay about their product or program. His point is that if you write at length, you have to think first, and he feels the quality of thought you have to do to write at length is greater than the quality of thought to put a PowerPoint together." – *Columnist Ezra Klein on Jeff Bezos buying the Washington Post*

pragmatic, *adj*. Realistic; reasonable. What businesses demand and Congress abhors. "Fix our collapsing bridges?" the senator whines. "Let's get real."

praise, *v*. When received, a simple "thank you" is sufficient. The thank you is like the stage actor's humble bow to the appreciative, applauding audience.

"If each of us were to confess his most secret desire, the one that inspires all his plans, all his actions, he would say: 'I want to be praised.'" – *E.M Cioran*

prayer, *n*. What you have going in to negotiate with a Fortune 500 company – and what you leave without.

"Even the cry from the depths is an affirmation: why cry if there is no hint of hope of hearing?" – *Martin Marty*

pre-call plan, *n*. It's like preparing for a job interview. It's what your visiting regional sales manager asks to see as you're driving to your first appointment. Not to worry. No one ever has one. Just sounds like a good thing to ask for.

"Write down your objectives on this first call (e.g. don't do anything stupid to get eliminated). Write down theirs (to eliminate you). What are you going to do to remember everyone's names? Write down everything you know and don't know about the prospect: who are they doing business with; why; what are they buying; how much are they paying; who made the decision to go with them; who influenced that decision. Write down what questions you think they want to ask you, and what questions you want to ask them. Write down the body language you're looking for. What's their personality and how can you use that knowledge? What handshake did they use and what does it mean? Write down what you think will happen; what you want to happen. Write down your next step at the meeting's conclusion. (What you don't know is what you're looking for.)" – *Jerry Hocutt*

precedent, *n*. A diplomatic way to say, "You're screwed because we've been screwing everyone else and been getting away with it."

"Let's find a way to deny this request so we can set a new precedent." – *State claims adjuster**

prediction, *n*. Future guesses you may not want to bet the house on. In 2014, the Denver Broncos were predicted to beat the Seattle Seahawks by 2.5 points in Super Bowl XLVIII. They lost by 35.

"No flying machine will ever fly from New York to Paris." – *Orville Wright, 1908*

Words That Escaped Me Before My Brain Finished Downloading

premonition, *n*. Told you so. (See *prediction*:)

"Gamblers wagered a record $119.4 million at Nevada casinos on Super Bowl XLVIII, allowing sportsbooks to reap an unprecedented profit ($19.4 million) as the betting public lost out in Seattle's rout (43-8) of the Peyton Manning-led Denver Broncos. That's millions more than the last three Super Bowls combined." – *ESPN*

prepare, *v*. Preparation is proof of commitment. Winning without it is just luck.

"The will to prepare is more important than the will to win." – *Bud Wilkinson, three time national champion football coach, University of Oklahoma*

presentation, *n*. An oral book report for adults. Stay calm. Take three deep breaths. Visualize everyone in the room as naked. Try not to get excited.

president, *n*. If he has a bodyguard entourage and Marine helicopters sitting on your company's lawn, you're looking at the President of the United States. If he makes more money than POTUS, he's your boss.

"Everyone please step back away from the windows. No one is allowed near the windows until Marine One takes off." – *White House tour guide herding guests away from the windows in the Blue Room as the president boarded his ride on the South lawn**

press release, *n*. Tidings of joy meant to start a buzz that no one cares about except the author. It's like parents sending out birth announcements.

pressure, *n*. What makes the popcorn pop, the champagne cork explode, and keeps you awake at night.

"I can't stand pressure." – *Job applicant's response to manager when asked to name her biggest weakness**

principal, *n.* Office visited by most every middle school boy at least once, preceded by the teacher's threat: "Boys! Quit playing with your Kendamas or I'll send you all to the principal's office right now!" A business principal is the decision maker the gate-keeper tells you is not in when she is.

pro forma, *adj.* Carried out as a formality to keep your job. Listening to the boss tell the same stories over and over again. (Lip-synching is a big no-no.)

probability, *n.* The chances the expert isn't; the plane is late; the traffic is jammed; the appointment cancels; the deal falls through; the books don't balance; the costs increase; your budget's been cut; your phone's not charged.

probably, *adv.* Doubtful; highly unlikely. "We'll probably complete the remodeling in a couple of weeks," said the contractor.

probably not, *adv.* Likely. "This won't get me in trouble, will it?" he asked. "Probably not," she replied with a wink and a smile.

probing, *v.* Uncomfortable procedures performed behind closed doors in the doctor's office. But in business it's the asking of questions. Not quite so invasive and uncomfortable, but the objectives are the same: to find the problem so the proper diagnosis can be made and remedies prescribed.
   "Does that hurt?" – *Dentist putting ice cube on tooth needing a root canal and sending patient through the roof**

problem analysis, *n.* A study of the customer's problem to see if the salesperson's solution is a fit. Even if it isn't a fit, if it's close enough, good enough.

problems, *n.pl.* The labor pains of knowledge, solutions, change, and evolution. Why businesses exist. Problems solved from the past include: how to light up the night; how to talk with someone across the country; is the moon really made of cheese?

"So I'll summarize: it's your problem, not mine." – *House, M.D.*

process, *n*. The nitty-gritty of how sausage is made that no one wants to be involved with. Like finding new customers through cold calling.

"If you can make the process fun – make the practices something the players will look forward to – you'll get better participation, the kids will learn faster, and their skills will dramatically improve." – *Texas high school football coach**

procrastinate, *v*. Wait a minute. I'll come up with something.

"Procrastinate now?" – *Unknown*

procrastinator, *n*. A pessimist trying hard to be an optimist.

"Just my luck. Maybe if I give it a couple of more hours it will go away." – *A man with chest pains*

product, *n*. A product is a tangible item, something you can touch or hold, like a computer or car. A service is an intangible, like legal advice or health insurance. Some people sell both the product and service in one item like a mobile phone (tangible item) that you can talk on (wireless service). Retail clerks sell products while delivering fast and courteous service. Politicians provide neither a product nor a service yet still get paid. Weird.

profit, *n*. The company's blood. When drained, companies become vampires looking for "mergers" with other companies in order to suck the profits out of them.

"Does it suck or bite to be a vampire?" – *Unknown*

promotion, *n*. A bump in pay, power, and prestige for the person who beat you out for it.

promotional product, *n*. A free giveaway to customers to help promote your company, brand, or product. Passed on to the customers' kids as gifts: "Look what I got for you at the trade show!"

"Would you like a kiss?" – *Attractive model working trade show booth giving out chocolate Hershey kisses**

proposal, *n*. Suggested products and prices the customer asks for from the vendor, which she has no intention of considering. Her mind was already made up weeks ago to go with her favorite vendor. She just needed a third one for show-n-tell with the boss.

prospect, *n*. Someone in need of your product, but still short on want. Needs a little more coaxing. It's like trying to get your cat to eat – anything.

protégé, *n*. The mentor's foil. Has dreams of benching her mentor, just as the NFL's number one draft pick connives to replace the aging 35-year old quarterback Billy "Gramps" McNaughton.

protocol, *n*. Proper procedures for how things are to be done so as to not offend anyone. For example, in business should men wait for the woman to extend her hand first when meeting, or is it okay for the man to take the initiative and extend his hand first?

"If a man would walk over and shake hands with another man, I expect him to walk over and offer his hand to me as well. Otherwise, he's not treating me as an equal and I'll hold it against him." – *Detroit woman business owner**

prototype, *n*. An original model; a Beta test; experimental. A model to work out all the kinks before production of multiple models. Like the first child in a family.

"She's our first child. And from the way things are going, she'll be our last." – *Flustered mom to friend*

prove it, *v.t*. Surest way to close the sale.

"This is the most durable china you'll ever see. Watch. I can drive a nail into this board with this coffee cup." – *Salesman closing the deal with husband and wife**

psychology, *n*. Mind games of influence and persuasion by using words or body language to affect beliefs and behaviors. If the boss is standing beside her desk, both hands on hips, and feet spread shoulder width apart (the "peacock" stance), her message is dominance, authority, and intimidation.

publicity, *n*. Anything that attracts attention. It's been said there is no bad publicity. Not said by Mitt Romney, featured in the infamous "47%" video.

"Sixty-seven seconds undid $1 billion in political ads." – *David Corn*

puddle jumper, *n*. In aviation, a two seat wide, twenty row, fixed winged aircraft that barely clears the treetops at the end of the runway. Frequent flyers to small towns find this is a great way to remove any bowel obstructions.

"We would like all passengers at the back of the plane to please move forward to the front seats to help distribute the weight of the plane for a safer takeoff." – *Flight attendant on Trans-Texas Airways (a.k.a. Tree Top Airlines) to Air Force recruits flying out of Dallas Love Field (1968) on way to basic training in San Antonio; instructions had to be repeated at stopovers in Waco and Austin after picking up more recruits**

pull a few strings. How a less qualified person beat you out for the position. How the old boys' network can yank you around. What Buffalo Bob did to Howdy Doody.

pull the trigger. It's when you've run out of excuses and have to pick up the phone to make the first cold call of the day. It could be worse. You could hear those words when standing in front of the firing squad.

"There comes a moment when you have to stop revving up the car and shove it into gear." – *David Mahoney*

puppy dog close, *n.* A sales technique that puts the product in the prospect's hands for a trial period to show friends and family and to instill feelings of ownership, while at the same time creating guilt for wanting to return it. Like what hospitals do with mothers of newborns.

purchase order, *n.* A legal offer to purchase specified products or services which requires acceptance by the seller to create a legal contract. It becomes the first step of turning the order into cash. It's like giving your friend an I.O.U. (offer) with a promise to pay $400 for his ski equipment after your next payday. Once he turns the equipment over to you (acceptance), you have a binding contract where you'll have to pay up.

push-back, *n.* A challenge from the customer that the statement you made doesn't hold water. It's when the natives challenged the Pilgrims who told them they were "just visiting".

qualified lead, *n*. A prospect worth meeting. A little better than a blind date.

qualify, *v*. How salespeople weed out legitimate buyers from looky-loos. How management evaluates and compares résumés. It's like an SAT entrance exam for customers and job applicants.

"Are you worth talking to for the next 10 minutes?" – *Peggy Klaus*

qualifying questions, *n.pl*. A battery of about seven critical questions asked by the salesperson to make sure he's talking with a prospect and not a suspect. Start with the easiest questions first and build to the most difficult questions last. Once the prospect starts answering he can't stop himself, and he can't help but dig a deeper hole that he can't get out of.

"Never lie in bed at night asking yourself questions you can't answer." – *Charlie Brown*

questions, *n.pl*. It's been said there are no stupid questions. That's stupid.

"The answer to this last question will determine if you're drunk or not: was Mickey Mouse a cat or a dog?" – *Unknown*

quid pro quo, *n*. Let's trade favors. "If you'll share your cab to midtown, I'll pay the fare." Usually a pretty good deal.

"I saw this guy hitchhiking with a sign that said 'Heaven'. So I hit him." – *Steven Wright*

quit, *v*. If you feel you must, ask one more question before making a final decision: "Is it still possible?"

"Courage in its simplest form: you do what you have to do, day after day, and you never quit." – *Eric Greitens, Navy SEAL*

quota, *n*. The minimum number of widgets a salesperson must sell to keep the job. Arbitrary number that comes to management in dreams. Unlike service, support, marketing, bookkeeping, and administrative positions, sales is the position where results can be measured objectively and are a direct result of the salesperson's efforts. All other positions are subjective with more lenient criteria (personal feelings, prejudices, politics) used to determine if the employee keeps the job. For example, if the sales numbers are not met this quarter, the office manager's job is not in jeopardy. It's like the wide receiver who must catch forty-five passes each season to stay on the team.

R

radio clock alarm, *n*. It's that alarm next to your bed in the hotel room that you keep waking up to check every hour because you don't know if you were able to set it right. Sometimes you even forget what time zone you're in and re-set the clock's time for the zone you came from. Don't even get me started with what happens when you're in another city and time changes from daylight savings to standard time the next morning. Not to mention that some states – even parts of states – don't have daylight savings times.

"I have two travel alarm clocks, the hotel's alarm clock radio, and I leave a wake-up call the night before when I have to do a presentation the next morning." – *Jerry Hocutt*

rainmaker, *n*. Someone who makes things happen. "I need three volunteers to work on this project – you, you, and you." That would be your boss.

"The haves and the have-nots can often be traced back to the dids and the did-nots." – *D.O. Flynn*

ramp-up, *n*. Get with it people. When management tells the sales team to ramp-up their sales, that's managespeak for "my bonus is on the line."

rant, *v.* What you do when assembling IKEA furniture. What the boss is on when the numbers are missed. What the salesperson does to protest her chargebacks. Your kids take it up a notch with a rant *and* rave.

read between the lines. To see what's not there. To hear what's not said. To understand without knowing.
   "Smart is when you believe only half of what you hear – brilliant is when you know which half." – *Unknown*

ready, *v.t.* Getting started doesn't require you to be ready. It requires a deadline. Then you'll start, ready or not.
   "Play ball!" – *Home plate umpire*

real reason. There's a reason people do things. And then there is the real reason. The salesperson's challenge is to dig down and find the real reason. One word should do it: "Oh?" If the customer gives an objection to your pitch, don't argue and don't justify. The first reason is not real. Simply respond, "Oh?" The second reason comes out. "Oh?" Then the next. And the next. Finally, the real reason will present itself with something like this: "I guess what I'm really saying is...." Ta-da!
   "The customer kept giving me reasons why the competitor's deal seemed better. My only response was 'Oh?' After five or six reasons I learned my competitor's price, the product (apples v. oranges) he was recommending, and the delayed delivery time because it was a foreign manufacturer. I pointed out the differences and closed the deal." – *President of a Seattle steel manufacturer**

realistic, *adj.* A word removed from the visionary's vocabulary.
   "If it's possible, it's not impossible." – *The Hour*

reality check, *n.* Looking at your losing Powerball lotto ticket and realizing another week has passed when you can't tell your boss to "Take this job and shove it." Also your paycheck.

really, *adv*. Guess not.
"You wearing that? Really?" – *Mom to teenage daughter**

reasons, *n.pl*. Motivations. Emotional reasons are more persuasive than logical ones. "Win one for the Gipper!" Not, "We're down by twenty-one. Run harder!"
"I was successful not because I was better – but because I was there." – *Walter Cronkite*

recall, *v.t*. Selective memory activity from witnesses and politicians that requires interpretation by the listener. "I don't recall saying that" translates into "I remember saying it, but I'm not admitting to it."

receptionist, *n*. A company's first impression to the outside world. Many are voicemail systems with more menus than the Cheesecake Factory; a model for how to lose customers by turning frustration into anger into searches for competitors.

recommend, *v.t*. When the boss asks what you would do, to see what you have learned.
"What would you tell our salespeople who say they don't have the time to cold call? And why would you insist they make their own cold calls instead of hiring telemarketers?" – *Business owner interviewing sales manager candidate**

recommendation, *n*. Suggested, not mandatory. The guy riding your bumper thinks speed limit signs are merely recommendations.

red flag, *n*. It's airport security stopping your bag going through the x-ray and the agent calling over her supervisor to take a look. Both look up at you suspiciously. You start to worry that the rubber chicken you packed for your presentation at the conference might look funny to them. It does. They start laughing. You're free to go.

red herring, *n.* Something to distract from the real issue. "Don't pay any attention to the neighbor's sinkhole next door. Just look at that magnificent view of the ocean from the front deck," the real estate agent sighs.

referral, *n.* The best compliment you can get and give.

reinvent, *v.t.* To take a product you're considering dumping and tweaking it to see if it can be salvaged after all. It's like renewing your wedding vows when you almost got divorced but didn't.

rejection, *n.* A test of your belief in what you're doing. J.K. Rowling received twelve rejection slips from publishers for her first *Harry Potter* book. Look where that got her.

relationship selling, *n.* It's like dating – you first want to see if you have something in common before taking it to the next level and then to the next before deciding if you'll commit to each other.

relevant, *adj.* What seemed important at the time, but over time it wasn't. "I really needed that job. But they gave it to someone else. That motivated me to start my own business."
 "Nothing in life is as important as you think it is when you are thinking about it." – *Daniel Kahneman*

respect, *n.* If you have to demand it, you have not earned it, nor do you deserve it.

response, *n.* Whoooo cares!
 "New grandparents are concerned with the 'naming' thing: what should our kids call us? I prefer the response of my friend Peter Osnos. 'Call me Elvis. What do they know?'" – *Tom Brokaw*

responsibility, *n.* Proof of confidence and leadership.
 "The buck stops here." – *Harry S. Truman*

results, *n.pl.* What happened because of what you did – or didn't do.

"All that we are is the result of what we have thought." – *Buddha*

résumé, *n.* HR spam. A pack of lies prettied up.

reward, *n.* Motivation to others to find something you can't: a business owner's commission to salespeople to find new business; the FBI's Most Wanted list. Also, a bribe to children to spend the night with their grandparents so mom and dad can have a date night.

RFQ, *n.* Request for Quote. In government, a requirement to establish a sense of fairness before awarding the contract to the already favored vendor before the RFQ was sent out. In business, the technique used by customers to let the vendor know he's in competition with others, so he better come in with his best price.

rifle approach, *n.* Unlike the shotgun approach, this approach is used where the target area you're marketing to is narrowly defined – much like drone strikes.

"My market is expectant mothers, mothers of newborns, and those who know them." – *Seattle business owner who designs baby albums and journals**

rigged, *v.t.* Magic tricks. Political parties suppressing votes. Records set by athletes using PEDs.

"M.L.B. Suspends Rodriguez and 12 Others for Doping." – *New York Times headline*

right, *n.* What men never are even if they are. Ask the women who know them.

"If a man says something in the woods and there are no women there, is he still wrong?" – *Steven Wright*

risk aversive, *n*. The trapeze artist who will never make it to the big top because she won't let go of her security. The salesperson who won't get out of her comfort zone to make the calls.

"Life shrinks or expands according to one's courage." – *Anais Nin*

road warrior, *n*. Businesspeople who travel extensively, are identified by the unchecked bags under their eyes, and can fit everything into one overstuffed carry-on (the reason you don't have room for yours in the overhead).

robocall, *n*. Political phone spam.

"We've written the laws for the Do Not Call Registry to stop those nuisance cold calls to your home. Of course, we've excluded political calls because they're important to solicit donations." – *Congressional member*

rocket science, *n*. Eliminating the pop-ups, malware, viruses, and garbage your kids put on your computer when they were on it.

ROI, *n*. Return on Investment. What parents pray for as they send their kids off to college.

role-play, *v*. Next to cold calling, role-plays are the most despised activity of salespeople because they're delusional. They assume salespeople have someone to sell to. Talking with customers, handling objections, and making presentations is easy. The reason salespeople fail is not because they don't know what to say, it's because they have no customers to sell to. Classes on how to overcome their own sales related psychological hang-ups, knowing how to find new business, and being improvisational would produce far more sales.

"I could sell to anyone – if I could just get in front of them first." – *Boston saleswoman*

rude, *adj*. Boorish bullies. It's the person who talks over you and won't let you make your point.

"People who think they know everything are very irritating to those of us who do." – *Unknown*

rule of thumb, *n*. The person who asks the questions controls the conversation and controls what the other person thinks about.

"We're thinking of going with your competitor. Why should we stay with you?" – *Customer to saleswoman**

rules, *n.pl*. Invisible fences to keep you inside the box.

rumor, *n*. A contagious viral lie. To avoid any blowback that could later haunt you, best not to let anyone know you were the virus's carrier. Even better, don't be caught on video saying it.

"I believe there's about 78-81 members of the Democrat Party who are members of the Communist Party." – *Former one-term Congressman Allen West, April 2012, before being turned out by the voters*

S

sale, *n*. What's lost on shoplifters.
    "Going to jail sale." – *Yard sale sign*

sales, *n*. A profession where every day is like job hunting, and every sales call is like a job interview.

sales call, *n*. It's like an archaeological dig – a process of discovery – where you never know what you'll find.
    "'Do you find things you're looking for?' asked Adelinho. 'Sometimes,' replied archaeologist Louise. 'Sometimes I find things I didn't know I was looking for.'" – *Kennedy's Brain*

sales cycle, *n*. The period of time it takes from finding a prospect to closing the deal. The same cycle people surfing dating websites go through.

sales expert, *n*. Someone who can persuade you to do something you don't want to do. Your baby with poop in his diaper.

sales force, *n*. A team of rivals.

"I told the traffic warden to go forth and multiply, though not exactly in those words." – *Woody Allen*

sales forecast, *n*. Blowing smoke.

sales improv, *n*. Every sales or job interview situation is improvisational: nothing can be scripted, surprises will be many, and you'll have to roll with the punches.

"Mother turning on the porch light and telling her daughter who's kissing her date goodnight: 'Honey – your husband's on the phone.'" – *Unknown*

sales interview, *n*. An awkward dance between the prospect and the salesperson. The prospect is not looking for reasons to do business with the salesperson, but for reasons to eliminate him from consideration. The salesperson is trying to pry confidential information from the prospect to see if she's a legitimate buyer. Both try not to say or do anything stupid. Good theater.

"Watching Governor Rod Blagojevich jog is like watching a stork in tights trying to gallop." – *Maureen Dowd*

sales manager, *n*. Tough job. You implement decisions made from above, you mediate conflicts between departments, and you motivate salespeople who don't want to be there. It's a lot like being asked to lead the parade while assigned as the scooper to follow the elephants at the rear of the procession.

sales pitch, *n*. An argument of *why's*: why your service or product can solve the customer's problem; why you're different; why your company is better than the competitor; why the price is right. The same pitch you made in your job interview to get hired.

sales posse, *n*. The sales team.

"Somebody once did a painting of our sales department. It was a still life." – *Unknown*

sales psychology, *n*. Mind games to influence, persuade, and control. "Follow me," the car salesman says to the buyers on the lot as he turns his back to them and walks towards the showroom. If the buyers follow, the salesman will soon have them on a test drive.

sales reports, *n*. Management's way of monitoring salespeople's activities in order to give them more guidance. Salespeople don't turn them in for two reasons. First, management never follows through to give guidance. Second, the salespeople want to hide the information on their customers as payback because they had to sign "no compete" contracts. If a salesperson leaves unexpectantly, management doesn't know where to start looking for their customers and prospects to save them fast enough.

sales resistance, *v.i.* The customer's way of playing hard to get while still wanting to be courted and caught.

"I need an answer. You won't hurt my feelings if you tell me 'no'. But we both need to get on with our lives." – *A New Jersey top producing saleswoman's closing tactic when dealing with procrastinators**

sales support, *n*. Administrative workers who assist the sales team when they're not wanting to kill them for making their work impossible.

sales tips, *n.pl*. Bite-size nuggets of information that can change behavior, influence sales, and improve skills. Advice given by one salesperson in the hallway to another who is on her way to an appointment.

"Looking for the solution without listening to the problem is like working in the dark." – *Advertisement*

"If someone's ankles are crossed as you're speaking, chances are they're either hiding something, holding something back, or have a negative attitude about what you're saying. Stop talking and ask, 'Do you have some ideas about this? I'd like to hear your opinions.' When they begin to speak they will uncross their ankles. Change their body language to change their attitude." – *Jerry Hocutt*

sales training, *n.* Unnecessary since "anybody can sell"; just as Chinese language classes aren't necessary since anybody can speak.

salesmanship, *n.* The art of selling that looks like Picasso's "cubist" paintings: you have an idea what it is, but you wouldn't swear to it.

salesperson, *n.* What no one sets out to be but becomes, because they don't know what else to do with their lives or their diplomas.

"I went into sales instead of practicing law because in sales you can be aggressive and go out and find new business. A lawyer has to build his practice over years by waiting for clients to come to him." – *Successful University of Texas Law School graduate selling insurance**

sample, *n.* A small teaser of the product given to prospects in hopes they'll buy the whole package. Much like a first date kiss.

sarcasm, *n.* Biting thoughts you can't hold in any longer.

"Toning down my sarcasm is yet another great piece of advice from you." – *Cal FitzSimmons*

scam, *n.* Rip-off. Concession stands at professional sporting events. Additional fees for exit row seats on the plane or for getting to board early.

scandal, *n*. What you stumbled upon that guarantees your early promotion and hefty raise. Congratulations!

scapegoat, *n*. Billy's innocent black sheep brother. The fall guy who had nothing to do with it. Ironic, but the accuser doesn't want the goat the same room at the time of the shearing; even better, that the goat's on a mountaintop in a faraway place.

"Call off the search. It appears the Mariners scapegoat has been located." – *The Seattle Times on upper-management passing the buck to the "bottom of the power spectrum" – the manager*

"A mountain goat is a hillbilly." – *Unknown*

schmooze, *v*. A company's all-employee booze cruise with the intention of building camaraderie. Backfires because with too much booze, loose lips sink ship.

screw up, *v*. The hotel giving your conference a ballroom next to a middle school graduation ballroom where the kids play fun and games all day using 5000 watt speakers.

"I bet you didn't know your competitors were attending the seminar and were shocked by the lack of control your staff had over the kids next door. I'm sure they'll bring this up when competing with you for future business." – *Hoarse speaker at the end of the day to the Long Island sales manager of an international hotel chain**

screwed, *v.t*. The lie has been discovered.

"If you were me, would you believe you?" – *Prime Suspect*

screwed up, *n*. What you're thinking of your last interview as you're driving away. Title of your autobiography. The type of people a psychologist needs to stay in business.

"What I should have said is nothing." – *Unknown*

script, *n.* Used by actors, Presidents, and telemarketers. They're like a map: they give you a starting point, an ending point, and give you several ways to get there. When cold calling, salespeople need three: one for the principal, one for the gatekeeper, and one for voicemail.

"Scripts are good because they force you to think about what you're saying, why you're saying it, and how to say it to influence others with the fewest words. They give you confidence, but shouldn't be read verbatim – only used as a guide to accomplish your task." – *Jerry Hocutt*

secret agenda, *n.* A hidden trap spoken by one without moving his lips. It's when he encourages you to "lay all our cards on the table" while hiding an ace up his sleeve.

secrets, *n.pl.* What everyone tries to keep – and steal. Inside information that, if shared with the wrong people, could get you a visit from the feds. Whispers indicate the secrets are about you.

"He that has eyes to see and ears to hear may convince himself that no mortal can keep a secret. If his lips are silent, he chatters with his fingertips; betrayal oozes out of him at every pore." – *Sigmund Freud*

security line, *n.* After boarding the plane you realize that's where you left your phone, your iPad, and your shoes.

self-fulfilling prophecy, *n.* Not finding that parking space close-up front like you knew you wouldn't. As you're halfway down the aisle you see in the rearview mirror a car pulling out where you just passed, and another car pulling in (the driver of which found the parking space close-up front like she thought she would).

self-starter, *n.* Low-maintenance workers with good work ethics who can motivate themselves to do what needs to be done, when it needs to be done, and do it right. What employers look for. Good luck with that.

"52% of workers 'are not into' their jobs; 18% are 'actively disengaged' from their jobs (having a 'permanent case of the Monday's'); and only 30% are 'into' their jobs." – *2013 Gallup Poll*

self-talk, *n.* Talking to oneself to find an answer to a nagging question, to solve a problem, or to give encouragement. Turns nasty when you start arguing with yourself.

"I always have a good listener when talking to myself." – *Unknown*

sell, *v.* Convincing others to believe that doing what *you* want them to do is in *their* best interest. Everyone – everyone – sells every day. Infants cry to get fed. Teens promise to stop whining if they can get the latest fashions. Parents assure their kids that a Yellowstone vacation will be more fun than Disney World. Teachers persuade students that geometry can actually help them in the real world. The salesperson sells the client that the product is a necessity. The client sells the salesperson that the price is too high. The boss must convince the employees that the goals are attainable. The service manager wins the case that the customer is at fault. The barista sells the new blend as a must try. The flight attendant demands that seat belts must be buckled. The attorney sells the jury that his client is innocent. The jurors sell each other on their beliefs. The dentist sells the parents on the need for their kid's braces. The doctor convinces the patient the tests are necessary. The running back sells the fake. Magicians trick to create belief in magic. Comedians exaggerate to sell the laugh. Actors use emotions to make the audiences laugh and cry. Writers sell mystery, intrigue, love, and war to entertain. The clergy uses guilt to get parishioners to walk the straight and narrow. Politicians sell their constituents they should be elected. Lobbyists bribe politicians for their special interests. The President sells the nation that stricter gun control laws are needed. The NRA lobbies they're not. Nations threaten war to keep the peace. Everyone sells. No exceptions.

selling, *v.* The heart and art of selling is the ability to find the people to sell to. Nothing else – service, product, pricing, presentations, handling objections, negotiating, closing – is important until you have someone to sell to.

selling tools, *n.pl.* Tools of influence and persuasion often misused, if used at all. Such tools include (but are not limited to): listening, body language, questioning, remembering names, decision making, speaking, and writing. Master the tools of sales just as the artist masters the canvass, colors, and lines.

"Don't shake your finger at someone if you're trying to make a point. It's like beating them over the head with a club." – *Allan Pease, body language expert*

seminar, *n.* Where employees go because they're made to go. They report back "I didn't learn a thing" without telling the boss they spent the entire time outside the meeting room on their phone.

"I learn by going where I have to go." – *Theodore Roethke*

send a message. A warning shot across the bow that the next shot could sink you. It's Steve Jobs personally pulling Apple's millions of dollars of ads from Fox News because of what he said was the "biased ideology of its commentators".

"Boys, if you try to go around me again, I'll cut you off at the knees!" – *Protective gatekeeper to two salesmen trying to find another way to get to her boss**

sense of humor, *n.* A funny stress reliever.

"I've always wanted to be somebody, but I see now I should have been more specific." – *Lily Tomlin*

sense of urgency, *n.* Recognition that a tipping point has arrived. The event will focus the mind and dictate the actions required. What's going to happen will happen with or without you, so you better be a part of it if you want to influence the outcome.

   "We got 'em right where we want 'em." – *Denver Broncos guard Keith Bishop to his teammates in the huddle as they started "The Drive" on their own two yard line, down by seven, in the 1987 AFC Championship game in Cleveland. Quarterback John Elway would drive them ninety-eight yards to the tying touchdown with thirty-seven seconds remaining. (Denver won the game in overtime by a field goal.)*

seriously, *adv.* A statement of disbelief that such an idiotic thing could be allowed to happen. Seriously?

   "I can't return the car until your managers open the gates when they get here at 8:00? Seriously? It's 6:00 now. My plane leaves at 7:30. Really? Seriously?" – *Response to shuttle driver outside locked gates at a St. Louis airport national car rental company**

service department, *n.* Where you take your product to get fixed because you didn't bother reading the instructions.

service person, *n.* Who salespeople are warned against taking with them on a sales call because they volunteer too much information that can kill the sale.

   "Let the silence suck out the truth." – *C.I.A.*

settlement, *n.* Hush money. The defendant knows he's guilty, but pays the plaintiff off so he won't have to say it out loud.

   "The NFL reached a $765 million settlement over concussion-related brain injuries among its 18,000 retired players. One of the principal terms of the settlement is that the agreement 'cannot be considered an admission by the NFL of liability, or an admission that plaintiffs' injuries were caused by football.'" – *ESPN*

severance package, *n*. For a fired executive, it's a payoff given to keep their mouth shut and not say what really happened.

shill, *n*. Kiss-ass decoy planted in the audience to generate false enthusiasm and excitement for the speaker who has no business being on the stage. What's that? That's your boss on stage? Nevermind.

shiny object, *n*. Anything that distracts you from doing your work. For example, any app for your tablet or phone.
 "Wow! That's 110 points!" – *Words with Friends player*

shock and awe. First-time visitor to New York City exiting the Lincoln Tunnel in his Newark airport rental car and somehow ending up driving down Broadway when he thought he was going to be on Long Island. Thanks MapQuest.
 "I will be where I am." – *Chief Joseph, Nez Perce*

short list, *n*. You're in the finals. You're either one of the best qualified or no one else wanted the job. Now you're confused and concerned.
 "I don't care to belong to any club that will have me as a member." – *Groucho Marx*

shotgun approach, *n*. Marketing technique that casts a wide net looking for prospects; like cluster bombing emails. No real qualified prospects sought, just anyone who will bite on the offer without much effort.

show-n-tell, *n*. Where the salesperson trots out the product, touches a few buttons, and waits for "Wow!" from the audience before telling what just happened. Bakeries by far have the best show-n-tells; no explanations needed and there's always a "Wow!"

showtime, *n*. The water broke. Get your act together – we're on!

"Never play peekaboo with a child on a long plane trip. There's no end to the game. Finally, I grabbed him by the bib and said, 'Look, it's always gonna be me!'" – *Rita Rudner*

sick days, *n.pl*. The days you come to work feeling really bad.

signature, *n*. On a contract, your word. On a doctor's prescription, illegible.

"Jack assures me that he is going to work to make at least one letter legible in order not to debase our currency should he be confirmed as Secretary of the Treasury." – *President Barack Obama when announcing Jack Lew's nomination and his reputation for having the worst signature on record*

silence, *n*. When words won't do.

"Silence can be so loud." – *James Lee Burke*

silver bullet, *n*. The answer to the long standing problem you've been wracking your brain over. Shocks you awake from a deep sleep at three in the morning.

simile, *n*. A figure of speech comparing two unlike things; usually using the words "like" or "as". Used to create an easy-to-see picture to avoid all the technical jargon. "This car is as fast as a bat out of hell!" See? You don't need to bring in a mechanic to dismantle the engine.

"I feel like a nail waiting to get hammered." – *Dilbert*

"Raising an infant is like being on suicide watch for the first three years." – *Michael J. Fox*

simple, *n*. Simple needs no explanations. Simple sells. A smile. A laugh. A touch.

"They say the world has become too complex for simple answers. They are wrong." – *Ronald Reagan*

sit down, *n*. Let's get together, put all our cards on the table, and put this thing to rest.

"Jamie's teacher called. She wants to have a 'sit down' with us. I don't like the sounds of this." – *Worried mom*

sitcom, *n*. It's walking out of your best customer's office and seeing – and then awkwardly greeting – your toughest competitor who's in the waiting area. And like most sitcoms, it's not funny.

"The best way to sell your car is to schedule five or six appointments at the same time for the people to stop by. They're all surprised to see the others there, and then they get nervous and want to make the buy before the other guy does. It also stops them from trying to negotiate the price down." – *College student who buys and then sells used cars from his off-campus home*

situation, *n*. Like the closing pitcher coming into the game with the bases loaded, you find yourself in a predicament you had nothing to do with, yet you have to save.

"If you can keep your head when all others about you are losing theirs, it's just possible you haven't grasped the situation." – *Jean Kerr*

skeletons in the closet. Send a novelty rubber skeleton to a customer who doesn't return your calls with this note written on the back of your business card: "This is me...waiting for you...to return my call."

"A skeleton walks into a bar and says, 'Give me a beer and a mop.'" – *Willie Nelson*

skill, *n*. What you acquire from correcting your mistakes.

"Mistakes – paying for your education." – *Unknown*

slippery slope, *n*. What you were told to avoid, didn't, and what cost you the promotion.

slogan, *n*. A short phrase that you hope will catch on and go viral. "Just do it." "Finger lickin' good!" "Got milk?" It's harder to write two or three catchy words than it is to write a novel.

slush fund, *n*. It's a lobbyist's slop in a pigsty where politicians love to grunt, roll around, and get filthy rich.
    "Oregon Farmer Eaten by Pigs" – *Time, October 2, 2012 (all they found left were his dentures and a few remains)*

small business, *n*. What started out as a big idea.

small talk, *n*. Talking without saying anything.
    "How do you talk for one minute without ever using the letter 'A'? Count 1-100. You won't use 'A' until you get to 101. And no matter how fast you count, you'll never reach 100 in 60 seconds." – *Comedian Alan King*

smartphone, *n*. A rectangular, flat, pocket phone with a germ-saving screen that has texting, apps, maps, and games that ensures we never have to use it for its intended purpose and have to actually *talk* with another human being again. Please wash your hands before poking around on mine.

smoke and mirrors. How did you do that? Wall Street banks manipulating energy prices in the dead of night (when usage is low and the prices are cheaper), so that when morning comes energy companies and their customers are paying substantially more.
    "JPMorgan Agrees to Pay $410 Million in Power Market Manipulation Case," – *New York Times, July 30, 2013*

smoke screen, *n*. Lies and deception. Evasive answers; answering questions that weren't asked; answering a question with a question; doctored charts and graphs; meaningless statistics.

"Why do audiences pay good money to be lied to, tricked, and bamboozled by magicians who even tell you there is no magic, that it's all deception?" – *Jerry Hocutt*

smug, *adj*. Someone who knows a better secret than you. They probably have a list of the layoffs and, too late, you realize you're on it and they're not.

snarky, *adj*. A smug SOB.

social media, *n*. How the anti-social types prefer to communicate.

social media marketing. Fool's gold.

"Back in the 1600's, alchemists tried to turn iron, something common, into gold, something precious. It didn't work. Not once. And yet we remain in hot pursuit: 'There must be a way to convert Facebook Likes into actual sales.'" – *Rhymes with Orange*

social proof, *n*. Psychological tool of influence that states that if one person does it, it's okay for you to do it too. "If Jimmy jumps off the roof, does that mean it's okay for you to do it too?" Well...yeah!

Socrates, *n*. One of the world's greatest salesmen who sold his ideas not by telling, but by asking questions to help the students arrive at their own "Aha!" moment.

sold, *v*. Psychologists say customers would rather "buy" than be "sold". Better to tell your prospect, "My biggest customer bought the same copier you're considering" rather than, "I sold this copier to my best customer." This shows it was the customer's decision to buy, and not the salesperson's prowess in making the sale.

"Not the brightest bulbs in the pack. They sold the car for gas money!" – *Unknown*

sole source bid, *n*. Bid written by your competitor, but the customer won't confirm it because she needs three bids to make the process look legit. Do something better with your time – take in a movie.

solution, *n*. An answered prayer.
"'How did you see it?' asked the surprised Dr. Watson. 'I was looking for it,' replied Holmes." – *Sherlock Holmes*

south, *n*. It's the elephant graveyard of lost sales: no one really knows where it is, but that's where tanked sales go to die.
"The presentation went south when the president got up and left in the middle of it." – *Regional sales manager*

spam, *n*. Hawaii's favorite breakfast meat and the only known Hawaiian word with just one vowel. Junk mail without a stamp. Not the news you were looking for. Leaves a bad taste in your mouth.

speaker, *n*. A salesperson of ideas.
"Always be shorter than anyone dared hope." – *Lord Reading*

speaker phone, *n*. Shut the damn thing off and quit annoying everyone when you're in the waiting area of the airport you narcissistic ninny.
"Am I still on the speaker phone? Stop it! Take me off the speaker! Now! Or I'm hanging up!" – *Irritated wife to husband who refuses to take her off the speaker in the airport terminal**

special, *n*. How every customer should be made to feel after their new purchase. Most just feel abandoned.

specialists, *n.pl*. Expert witnesses who swear under oath that the other attorney's specialist is a hack.

speech, *n.* A group sale of ideas made by too many speakers who can't speak, can't sell, and have no ideas. That, and they're too long.

"Speeches are like babies – easy to conceive and hard to deliver." – *Pat O'Malley*

spiff, *n.* Salesperson's prize for selling a specific manufacturer's product that's usually a poor seller. Manufacturers bribe the salespeople with rewards to unload them, much like your best friend tries to unload her cousin on you. Caveat emptor!

"I don't care about the prize. It's a lousy product and I'm not going to push it on my customers. I have to live with my customers, not the manufacturer." – *Salesperson with integrity**

spin selling, *n.* It could have been worse. It's putting a happy face on a losing situation.

"Second Place: the first loser." – *Dale Earnhardt*

split the difference. A measure of your negotiating skills. The party winning the negotiation never suggests splitting the difference.

spontaneous, *adj.* Jumping in for your first swimming lesson because your boat is sinking.

square one, *n.* It's where you're sent back to start over again by your mistakes you weren't able to overcome. A good thing about those mistakes is they teach you the changes that need to be made. If you don't learn from your mistakes, it becomes *Groundhog Day*.

"Experience is the name everyone gives to their mistakes." – *Oscar Wilde*

stakeholders, *n.pl.* Those who have a stake in the enterprise's successful outcome and, better yet, can't back out of their commitment; passengers on the plane.

stalemate, *n*. It begins when the waiter delivers the check and no one reaches for it. You're stuck with it when the other party excuses herself to go to the ladies' room.

stalker, *n*. Salespeople walk a fine line between being persistent and being a stalker. To avoid a trip to the hoosegow, here's how to protect yourself: "I want to be persistent. I don't like giving up. But I don't want to wear out my welcome. I'll leave it up to you. Would you like me to keep in touch, or should I move on?"

"On my last call the prospect told me to stop calling. He said he thought I was a stalker, that I scared him, and to never call him again. But I think I'm infatuated with him. I know he's married, but I don't care. I keep calling and leaving messages, but he never calls back. What should I do?" – *Saleswoman in Texas we'll call "Pecan" because she's a nut**

stalker technique, *n*. If the customer doesn't respond to your overtures, send her a note made up of letters cut out from magazines with this message: "I know this seems creepy, but all I want is 15 minutes of your time."

"When I said 'Follow me', I meant on Twitter." – *Jerry Hocutt*

stall, *v*. To delay making a decision because you're hoping something will happen in your favor to make the decision easier. It won't and it won't.

"Nothing is more difficult, and therefore more precious, than to be able to decide." – *Napoleon Bonaparte*

Starbucks, *n*. Rent-free conference room for home based businesses. Off-site HR job interview locations where parties don't want to be found out what they're up to. A holding area for businesspeople early for their appointments.

"Like most Americans, I prefer to stir my coffee by shooting it repeatedly with a handgun that I keep concealed under my sport coat. Shoot-stirring is efficient, adds a nice gunpowdery taste and is far more environmentally friendly than those wasteful wooden stir sticks. Sadly, though, I can no longer bring my Browning Hi Power 9 mm pistol/latte frother into a Starbucks coffee shop. Company CEO Howard Schultz announced last week that guns are not welcome at any Starbucks location." – *Rex Huppke, Chicago Tribune, September 24, 2013*

static, *adj*. Stalled; not going anywhere. To create movement introduce new information, because new decisions will be required. "We're leaving. You coming with us?"

"Status Quo: Latin for the mess we're in." – *Jeve Moorman*

statistics, *n.pl*. Cherry-picked facts to support your position that are in conflict with your opponent's cherry-pickings.

"If there's an opinion, facts will be found to support it." – *Judy Sproles*

stepped in it. Crap!

stigma, *n*. A blemish on an otherwise sterling job interview performance.

"She showed up for an interview in the summer wearing a bathing suit. Said she didn't think I'd mind." – *AP*

story, *n*. "It was a dark and stormy night when, from the pit of Hell, a shrill, bone-chilling howl made the hair on the back of my neck stiffen, and then...." Salespeople should master stories when making presentations instead of drowning customers in facts, figures, and charts. Easier for customers to relate to, and easier for them to remember in order to tell your story to others.

"To make a long story short, there's nothing like having the boss walk in." – *Unknown*

storyboard, *n*. A simple sales prop that tells a story to make it easier and more fun to remember. "This little piggy went to market, this little piggy stayed home...."

strategy, *n*. The what, not the how. It's the goal to save $5000 in the negotiation. What you'll say, do, offer, and counteroffer is the how – the tactics.
  "Luge strategy? Lie flat and try not to die." – *Tim Steeves*

street cred, *n*. It's the person who has bounced back from their own failures, setbacks, and mistakes and can help to stop others from going down the same path.
  "A credible messenger has 'been there, done that'." – *Ameena Matthews*

street performers, *n*. Original, creative, and improvisational salespeople who know daily what they're worth. The best are in Times Square and at San Francisco's Fisherman's Wharf. The Naked Cowboy of Times Square: eight million people in the city and you'll remember one.
  "BOO!" – *The Bushman of Fisherman's Wharf jumping out from behind a portable bush he's squatting behind and scaring the living daylights out of unsuspecting lunchtime strollers while tourists stand aside to laugh and fill his tip jar**

stress, *n*. Pressure before it's released. Common stressors include bosses, deadlines, and kids.
  "I don't suffer from stress. I am a carrier." – *Unknown*

stretch of the imagination. The fine line between fact and fiction.
  "Is that what you know – or what you believe?" – *House, M.D.*

strip search, *n.* TSA job description. No plane is allowed to leave the gate until all passengers have been publicly humiliated. Pole dancing discouraged except in the lounge area.

struggle, *v.i.* The first chapter in every small business's story. The tale is always the same: exciting, painful, scary, humbling.
 "Be kind, for everyone you meet is fighting a hard battle." – *Philo*

subject line, *n.* Email's knock on the door. The first indicator of spam. There are smart ones and stupid ones – mostly stupid. The funny ones are best.
 "Gingrich think tank declares bankruptcy" – *Ron Judd*
 "Scalia arrested trying to burn down Supreme Court" – *The New Yorker's Andy Borowitz regarding Justice Scalia's 2013 scathing dissent of majority decisions handed down on gay rights cases*

subliminal persuasion, *n.* Invisible marketing to the invisible subconscious. You know it's working when you find yourself standing in line – again – to order another cinnamon dolce latte, extra hot, and don't know why you can't stop yourself.
 "I saw a subliminal advertising executive, but only for a second." – *Unknown*

subway, *n.* Best way for throngs of people to travel underground for great distances in New York City. In fact, the only way. All subway riders wear black to hide the dirt and soot from the underground platform assaults. Also, a sandwich that tastes like it was found on the floor on the rear car of the "D" train.

success, *n.* No universally accepted definition. What many call what they have had to settle for.
 "I couldn't wait for success, so I went ahead without it." – *Jonathan Winters*

The Wickedly Fun Dictionary of Business

suggested list price, *n*. A fake price to plant subconsciously that the product is more valuable than it really is.

suggestion box, *n*. Today's version is the link on a company's website or social networks: "Tell us what you think." They don't really care, so don't bother. It just provides amusement for their interns during their breaks. It also helps them increase their page views so they can charge more for advertising. They're simply letting you blow off steam so you'll feel like you did something important and they really care. You didn't and they don't. It's the same thing as contacting your congressman. Here's a suggestion: get a life. You've got better things to do.

supervisor, *n*. The middle manager with lots of responsibilities, but the most important is to be a punching bag that irate customers can go a few rounds with. "Who's your supervisor? Get your supervisor! I want to talk to her!"

"Caller: 'I don't like the lady taking reservations. She won't give me a free ticket to the program. I understand you're her supervisor. Well, the owner told me yesterday that I could get a free ticket.' Supervisor: 'Yes, I'm her supervisor, and (a) I'm also the owner; (b) I've never talked with you; and (c) the lady is my daughter.' Caller: click!" – *Shyster using intimidation trying to wrangle a freebie to our seminar (and who later snuck into the program without a ticket anyway)**

surprise, *n*. To be avoided in all negotiations.

"Because the hotel's sales manager didn't call back the next day as promised, and instead left for a two week vacation, when I called back and got her assistant I was able to save $800 by negotiating the price down for the same ballroom we used last year." – *Jerry Hocutt*

surrogate, *n*. A seat filler. "I need a volunteer to attend the meeting for me. Robert. You'll do."

survey, *n.* The magic word used to protect cold callers from violating the Do Not Call Registry. "This is not a cold call. I'm doing a survey. Would you like to buy 100 cans of Slippery Slimy Slug Spray?"

suspect, *n.* Not a criminal, but close. The lowest level of the three possible people who could buy your product: customer, prospect, suspect. It's criminal for them to waste your time because they're "just looking".

SVP, *n.* Senior Vice President. Carries the coat for the Executive Vice President and will quickly pass it off to the Vice President when the EVP isn't looking.

sympathy, *n.* "I feel your pain, man." Not to be confused with *empathy* which is "I understand your pain." If you feel like the other person, you're not in a position to help because both of you are miserable.

"They don't come to me for sympathy." – *Sherlock Holmes*

T

tact, *n*. Listening to your instincts and biting your tongue.

"The real art of conversation is not only to say the right thing at the right time, but also to leave unsaid the wrong thing at the tempting moment." – *Unknown*

tactics, *n.pl*. The steps required to produce the results. A cake recipe. The musical notes of a song. A football play.

"Happy people plan actions, they don't plan results." – *Dennis Wholey*

take it or leave it. Give up. Let me win or we'll both lose. A last-ditch negotiating tactic when all others have failed.

"The reason you like the idea of gaining $100 and dislike the idea of losing $100 is not that these amounts change your wealth. You just like winning and dislike losing – and you almost certainly dislike losing more than you like winning." – *Daniel Kahneman*

take the bait. A trial close. A test to see if you can hook a "live one" with a minimal offering. It's the airline offering a $50 coupon if someone will give up their seat on the overbooked flight before finally having to relent and give a free ticket because no one fell for it.

takeaway, *n*. What you learn the hard way.

"A man who carries a cat by the tail learns something he can learn in no other way." – *Mark Twain*

talk, *v*. A civil conversation between a boss and an employee where the boss speaks first: "I talk, you listen." An activity where many words are spoken, but none are heard. Wife to husband, "Hey! I'm talking to you!"

"I have less and less to say but I can't stop talking." – *David Letterman*

targeting, *v.t*. Marketing departments use targeting as a means of identifying prospects to develop their campaigns. Example for beer commercials: men, 25-35, single, irresponsible, silly, think they're studs. Example for Victoria's Secret: men, 25-35, single, irresponsible, silly, think they're studs.

tax audit, *n*. A colonoscopy of your books. Except with a real colonoscopy you get drugs and pictures.

"This shouldn't hurt much." – *Gastroenterologist**

taxes, *n.pl*. It's like a bank robbery where the government is the bandit and you're the banker. Stick 'em up!

"The hardest thing in the world is to understand the income tax." – *Albert Einstein*

taxis, *n.pl*. In New York, speeding, darting, mobile yellow coffins.

"Tourists, have some fun with New York's hard-boiled cabbies. When you get to your destination, say to your driver, 'Pay? I was hitchhiking.'" – *David Letterman*

teach, *v*. Teaching is learning twice.

"The best we can do is to show others what we have seen up to now. It's at best a progress report, a map of our experiences, by no means the absolute truth." – *Jon Kabat-Zin*

The Wickedly Fun Dictionary of Business

teacher, *n*. The best insist you learn rather than waiting to be told.

"I should have thanked him – for reminding me that it's not what the teacher says, but what the student hears that matters." – *Harvey Penick*

team building, *n*. The fostering of camaraderie with co-workers; sometimes carried out in remote, humid areas dense with mosquitoes and snakes – or in the ballroom at the Ritz. Warm fuzzy feelings of cooperation that last about one week until the cliques start clicking again.

"Get eleven men together and you'll have a football team. Get eleven women together and you have a riot." – *Maureen Dowd*

team selling, *n*. More theory than practice. It's more like an obstacle course with barriers that have to be negotiated and overcome internally and out of the customer's sight. The salesperson closes the sale. If billing doesn't get a clean A+ credit report, they'll kick it back as disapproved. Management doesn't want to give as big a discount as it takes to get the deal. Service will deliver and install on their schedule, not the customer's. And bookkeeping will invoice incorrectly. Go team!

"A team that believes is a lot more dangerous than a team with talent." – *TV sports announcer*

technique, *n*. Trick of the trade. For example, if you think someone is not being candid with you and is holding back critical information, you need to get her to relax and open up by simply asking, "Is there something else?" This shows her you're in no hurry, that you will allow her to calmly collect her thoughts, and you let her know she has a receptive listener who is trying to solve her problem and get a solution that works best for her. As the speaker expands on "something else" she will sometimes discover the solution in her own answers and give you credit for being so perceptive.

"When interviewing job applicants, it's best to come out from behind your desk and sit in a chair next to or across from the person you're interviewing. The desk is like a barrier making the interview appear to be more confrontational, and making it less likely that the applicant will relax and open up." – *Albuquerque general manager**

telecommute, *v.i.* Working from home with a computer, tablet, and smartphone. Not unlike being paid to be in solitary confinement.

"Computers make it easier to do a lot of things, but most of the things they make it easier to do don't need to be done." – *Andy Rooney*

telecommuter, *n.* Member of a remote tribe who has lost all human contact.

telemarketer, *n.* Good lead-generation telemarketers don't last long. Once they figure out they're doing the toughest thing in sales (cold calling) and are good at it, they insist on being put into outside or inside sales where they can not only find customers but earn the commissions on them as well.

"The best way to find a good telemarketer? Have applicants call in to your company's voicemail and sell you in thirty seconds on why you should make an appointment with them." – *California telemarketing manager**

telemarketing, *n.* The mother of the Do Not Call Registry.

"I have bad luck with women. A woman I was dating told me on the phone, 'I have to go, there's a telemarketer on the other line.'" – *Zach Galifianakis*

telephone cold call, *n.* Outgoing calls made by a telemarketer, inside salesperson, outside salesperson, or the Pope. One cold call every thirty minutes of each working day (244 working days per year) adds up to over 3800 cold calls in a year. That's probably

3700 more than you made all of last year. Now try convincing your boss you don't have the time to cold call.

"The Pope (Francis) – famous for picking up the phone and cold calling Catholics out of the blue – has done it again. This time he called an order of nuns in a convent in Spain to wish them Happy New Year. But no one answered and an apparently frustrated Pope left a message." – *CBS News, January 4, 2014*

temporary setback, *n*. It's the starter's pistol when she fires two quick shots. It doesn't mean the race can't be run, just that there was a false start and you have to go back and start over again. No biggee.

tentative, *adj*. Uncertain. Tentative is when management sets a new product release date with lots of hoopla, without realizing that engineering considers the date as only a moving target.

"In the face of uncertainty, there is nothing wrong with hope." – *Bernie Siegel, M.D.*

territory, *n*. The locus of a salesperson's customers. Guarded with extreme prejudice against her own company's poaching salespeople who sneak into her domain looking to bag a few customers.

"Park your car, get out, and walk. That's the only way to really understand your territory. I called on a tiny hole-in-the-wall office squeezed between two vacant buildings I must have driven by a hundred times. Ended up selling them eighty-five of our units the next week." – *Jerry Hocutt*

test market, *n*. Willing participants who volunteer to take part in a Beta test. Like drug companies testing on volunteer lab rats.

testify, *v*. What CEO's do when their products cause harm. The only time in life when memories – for some unknown reason – falter. I swear, my hand to God.

testimonial, *n*. They said it, not me. Testimonials should give specific facts and figures of the benefits your service or product has provided, and not generalities. "I used your handshake and body language techniques from your seminar on a sales call the next week and ended up making a $4000 sale!" Not, "I really liked your seminar. It was fun." If the happy customer procrastinates in sending the testimonial (or is embarrassed by her writing skills), it's okay for the salesperson to write it for her and send it to her for her approval and to make any changes. Get permission to use the customer's full name and company name to show it's legitimate.

"I asked a woman who had survived Auschwitz how she defines 'friendship'. She said her test was, 'would they hide me?'" – *Warren Buffett*

testimony, *n*. Lies by both sides – to the best of their recollection.

tête-à-tête, n. A private conversation between two people. It's like when the catcher is talking to the pitcher on the mound and both are covering their mouths with their gloves. Or when your boss is talking with your sales manager behind closed doors. Their next move will reveal what the conversation was about.

text messages, *n.pl.* Brief, abbreviated messages that read like vanity license plates. Biggest problem: how do you know when to quit responding so you won't look rude by quitting too soon?

"BLOND" – *Iowa license plate mounted upside down on the car*

texting, *v*. Wrds wtht vwls. (Why texting isn't big in Hawaii.)

"Dear Students: I know when you're texting in class. Seriously, no one just looks down at their crotch and smiles. Sincerely, Your Teacher." – *Sign posted in high school class*

therapy, *n*. Mind explorations.
"After a year of therapy, my psychiatrist said to me, 'Maybe life isn't for everyone.'" – *Larry Brown*

thinga-majiggy, *n*. It's that thing that always breaks. Funny thing is, the service department always knows what you're talking about.

think, *v*. Best done with your mouth shut so words won't escape you.
"Thinking is like loving and dying. Each of us must do it for himself." – *Josiah Royce*

thinking on your feet. Coming up with a good one when caught off guard. It's when you surprise even yourself with a plausible excuse why you're late for the meeting. "How did you come up with that?" asks one of your co-workers after the meeting. "I don't know. It just came to me."
"The best thinkers on their feet are pedestrians." – *Unknown*

thoughts, *n.pl*. What happens before before. A song before it's written. A word before it's spoken. A picture before it's painted.
"The ancestor of every action is a thought." – *Ralph Waldo Emerson*

threat, *n*. A promise you won't like, that follows "or else...!"

tick tock. Step on it. Time's not on your side.
"How you spend your time is more important than how you spend your money." – *Unknown*

tie, *n*. A tie – it's color or design, and whether it's a bow-tie, straight tie, string-tie, or bolo tie – is a barometer of how the wearer is feeling that day: conservative, liberal, flamboyant, festive, brash, formal. The absence of a tie in a normal tie-wearing situation is, likewise, a statement of the wearer; as is whether the tie is worn by a woman. So, maybe ties do serve a purpose other than being last minute Christmas gifts (which also makes a statement about the giver).

"The reason I wear different brooches with my dresses each day is to get people to notice them and start conversations with me so we'll have something fun to talk about. In effect, it's a 'soft' cold call where they actually initiate the contact." – *North Carolina businesswoman**

Tiffany's, *n.* Their name, reputation, and classy storefront help to disqualify prospective buyers by shaming anyone without money from entering.

"It's too expensive for you." – *Saleslady at exclusive Swiss boutique refusing to show Oprah Winfrey the Tom Ford Jennifer bag that sold for $38,000*

time, *n.* Killing time isn't murder – it's suicide.

"Take your time – but hurry." – *Wyatt Earp, when asked how to win a gunfight*

time management, *n.* Whatever time you thought you saved today, you lost by looking for your keys and wallet.

"Time would become meaningless if there were too much of it." – *Ray Kurzweil*

time zones, *n.pl.* Time travel that gives and takes time.

tip jar, *n.* Customer subsidized wages. Money jar next to the cash register to make customers feel guilty that they're not chipping in to the employees' pension plan. Much of the money has been put in by the store owner to give the impression that everyone tips. Instead of giving tips, half the patrons think the owners should be paying the workers higher wages. The other half think this is a good idea and return to their offices and put tip jars on their desks for doing the work they're paid to do anyway.

tipping point, *n*. It's your boss catching you red-faced and asking, "What the hell were you thinking?" Or it could be the point where you and your barstool awkwardly departed ways after one too many drinks at happy hour.

title, *n*. Good to have since people can't remember names, but they can remember titles. And if you have a name that's already a title it can lead to faster promotions; like Private Major Major in *Catch-22* who got promoted to Major Major Major in four days.

Toastmasters, *n*. Uh. Ah. Um. (Inside joke.)

tomorrow, *n*. Where hope lives.
"They say a person needs just three things to be truly happy in this world. Someone to love, something to do, and something to hope for." – *Tom Bodett*

top brass, *n*. Knuckle busters – nuns with rulers.

touché, *int*. Witty response. Customer: "I wouldn't do business with you if you were the last company on earth." Salesman: "Oh, yeah? Well, your mama wears army boots." Okay, maybe a little wittier.

trade out, *n*. It's when someone wants to trade his product for yours, knowing his product has no value to him or to you. Practiced with fervor between sports teams. "I'll trade you my 32-year old back-up quarterback for your second round draft pick."
"Got this car for my daughter...pretty good trade, huh?" – *License plate holder on a new SUV near a high school*

trade show, *n*. For vendors, exposure and a chance to check out the competition. Who knows? They may even be hiring. For visitors, an opportunity to stuff their goody bags with samples for Christmas regifting.

"Of salespeople working a trade show booth, only 8% will walk over and introduce themselves to visitors standing on the perimeter. Yet 76% of those visitors will become more open and talkative if they meet the salesperson, and 86% will remember the salesperson by name." – *AP*

tradition, *n*. Thinking inside the box.

train wreck, *n*. Disaster caused by missed or ignored signals. It's the service person volunteering too much information and not seeing her salesman vigorously shaking his head back and forth.

"She just got too lazy to shut up." – *Justified*

travel, *v*. The good thing about business travel is.... Well, it can be.... Anyway, sometimes it's.... Nevermind. Can't think of anything good that comes from it.

"My mom taught me about time travel. 'If you don't straighten up, I'm going to knock you into the middle of next week!'" – *Unknown*

traveling arm handshake, *n*. As you're shaking hands with the other person, your left hand touches them on their right forearm, and gradually travels to the upper arm, and then onto their shoulder. The touching of the left hand conveys emotions; the higher up the hand travels, the stronger the emotions. Meeting someone new, they don't like this as they feel you're trying to move inventory. Rule of thumb: unless it's a relative, keep your left hand to yourself.

trial balloon, *n*. An employee brought in from a temp agency.

trial close, *n*. A test close to see if the prospect is buying what you're selling before going in for the kill. Best trial closes have only one answer so the prospect is backed tightly into the corner.

"Would you like four wheels on your car, or is three good enough?"

trivial, *adj*. Insignificant; no big deal. What customers want you to believe when they ask for a tiny addition to the contract. "Of course, when you re-shingle the roof, you'll throw in a free skylight too, right?"

trust, *n*. Have a little faith and those you give it to will want to prove you are right in giving it to them.

"The minute you give people a lot of negative, beat-down stuff, in our case we thought our customers could feel it. What we tried to tell the salespeople is, 'We trust you, we're not going to tell you how to do it. We want you to come up with your own way to do it.'" – *John Nordstrom on why their department stores are well known for their first-class service*

trust me, *v.i.* En garde!

"Anybody who wants the presidency so much that he'll spend two years organizing and campaigning for it is not to be trusted with the office." – *David Broder*

trust your gut. A test of what you believe rather than what you know.

"Intuition is reason in a hurry." – *Holbrook Jackson*

truth, *n*. What sometimes pops out of kids' mouths unexpectantly that puts you in an embarrassing situation. What people try to hide if it's not in their favor. What country singers reveal with a twang.

"Country Music: three chords and the truth." – *Harlan Howard*

"It does not require many words to speak the truth." – *Chief Joseph, Nez Perce*

truth in advertising, *n*. Drug ads where they're required to tell you not just how their products will heal you, but how they'll kill you as well.

"Why go elsewhere to be cheated, when you can come here?" – *Sign in the window of an Oregon general store*

truthfully, *adv*. If followed by a question mark, the speaker is asking if you'd rather hear a better – albeit, still dishonest – version. "Truthfully?"

"Even with truth on your side, it can still be hard to make others believe you." – *Garfield*

try, *v*. What you do when you don't know what else to do.

"Trying is an action." – *House, M.D.*

TSA, *n*. Transportation Security Administration. Agents at the end of the Bin Laden shuffle line where passengers get frisked, searched, and groped. Some travelers like it so much they even return to the end of the line to have it done again. Some unseen agents take the added responsibility to open and examine your bags (not in your presence, of course) and to relieve you of any infected Apple products and jewelry that could snag your sweaters.

"My toddler grandson liked to suck on the face of my rubber fish (stage prop) I used in my seminars and would end up getting slobber in it that would squirt out if the fish was squeezed. As the TSA agent took it out of my carry-on and was inspecting it, I was praying she wouldn't squeeze it." – *Jerry Hocutt on leaving out of heavily guarded Newark airport shortly after 9/11**

twat, *n*. A SWAT tweet.

tweet, *n*. Nonsense, thankfully limited to 140 characters at a time. (This nonsense took 92.)

"Before tweeting people use to keep their thoughts to themselves." – *David Letterman*

twist, *v*. To put a positive spin on the horror story being spun, much like sci-fi and mystery writer Ray Bradbury. "Our hundreds of aircraft engineers did a fantastic job in saving our bacon on this project. But now we no longer need them, so they're all being laid off."

"Asking an aerospace worker if he's ever been laid off before is like asking a mother if she's ever had a baby." – *Richard Kapusta*

twit, *n*. A nitwit tweeter.

Twitter, *n*. A neurological disorder: "She's all a-twitter."

"Three strippers followed me on social media, I followed them back. Next thing I know I'm in the GM's office. Now I'm off Twitter." – *St. Louis Rams rookie receiver Tavon Austin speaking to a group of high schoolers*

two jobs, *n.pl*. This month's rent.

two seconds, *n*. According to Harvard psychologist Dr. Nalini Ambady, that's how quickly people are making accurate decisions about whether they like you, trust you, and believe you. Mostly starts with a handshake or a smile.

"Mitt Romney smiles like he's hiding a dead hooker in the trunk of his car." – *Comedian Greg Rogell*

two-faced, *n*. A friend who congratulates you with a slap on the back with a knife.

U

U.S. Post Office, *n*. Rumored new ad slogans being considered to increase their business and put a tourniquet on their bleeding red ink: "Have you ever *tried* doing business with the post office?" "Making the possible impossible." "Apathetic is how we roll."

"Where else can you give someone forty-six cents and say, 'Can you take this letter to Alaska for me?'" – *Kathleen Madigan*

ulterior motive, *n*. A bribe disguised as a campaign contribution.

"A proctologist is what you call a brain surgeon operating on a politician." – *Gary Wise*

ultimatum, *n*. No wiggle room: put all your seatbacks and tray tables in their upright and locked positions.

unbeliever, *n*. Proof – not persuasion – required. "Show me!" Missourians. The customer you can't close. A worker not committed to the mission.

unconscious, *n*. Not aware your boss is standing behind you while uploading your latest photos onto your social networks.

unconsciously competent, *n.* The highest level of competence. No conscious thought required. What you do has become habit. You know without even knowing how you know. It's the "franchise" quarterback with a sixth sense and split second timing who can scramble from danger. It's the sidewalk artist who can draw and talk to admirers at the same time. It's driving while talking with your passengers. (See *consciously competent, consciously incompetent, unconsciously incompetent.*)

unconsciously incompetent, *n.* The lowest level of competence. You're stupid and you don't know it. It's when someone asks you to name the ten Supreme Court Justices and you actually come up with ten names. (See *consciously competent, consciously incompetent, unconsciously competent.*)

under fire. A withering assault on your beliefs.
"We have women in the military, but they don't put us in the front lines. They don't know if we can fight, if we can kill. I think we can. All the general has to do is walk over to the women and say, 'You see the enemy over there? They say you look fat in those uniforms.'" – *Elayne Boosler*

under-the-table, *adj.* Where congressional business pays off. Where frat brothers are found at party's end.

unintended consequences. Didn't see that coming! Your mind leaving you thoughtless and alone without telling you it was going.
"Oops!" – *Embarrassed presidential contender, and Texas Governor, Rick Perry with his 53-second brain freeze unable to remember one of the three federal departments he wanted to abolish in a nationally televised GOP debate*

unique, *adj.* One-of-a-kind. What you'd like to clone but you can't because, well, it's unique.

Words That Escaped Me Before My Brain Finished Downloading

"How do you catch a unique rabbit? Unique up on it. How do you catch a tame rabbit? Tame way, unique up on it." – *Unknown*

unsell, *v.* Selling the competitors down the river by blessing them. "Snicker, Snicker, and Snort is a fine law firm, and their management – bless their heart – is working overtime to recover from their blunders that nearly landed them in Leavenworth doing hard time."

update, *n.* Whas' up?

up-sell, *v.* Walking through Sears in the mall to get to Nordstrom's.

upside, *n.* Positive turn to a downside event.
"The good thing about missing my flight and having to layover until the next day was that I ran across my buyer in the airport's gift shop and she gave me her first order." – *Washington small business owner**

USA Today, *n.* A traveler's fun newspaper that is colorful, full of pictures and graphics, and is a quick read. A grown-up's daily Weekly Reader.

user friendly, *n.* The product is so easy to use that instructions are not required. Like when the car salesman hands you the keys and tells you to take the Lamborghini for a spin around town. Or a kiss. Or a hug.

USP, *n.* Unique Selling Proposition. An advantage or benefit your product or company has over the competition.
"The president asked me, 'Why should I do business with your bank?' I told him, 'Because I work for them and not the competition.' I got the business." – *Austin banker**

V

vacation days, *n.pl.* Days off you accumulate but feel guilty about using. If you do use them, you wonder if your job will still be there when you return. Best not to use them for both reasons.

valuable, *n.* Something you don't want your competitor to have, for example, your best employees. Hurt, then worried, then scared when you find your competitor doesn't even want them.
  "I would never consider buying one of our competitors. I'd like to have their routes, but I don't want to inherit their people." – *Herb Kelleher, former CEO of Southwest Airlines*

value, *n.* Nothing has value until you want it. The more you want it and the more you have to compete to get it, the more valuable it becomes. That's the principle behind Christie's, Sotheby's, and eBay.
  "The reader will take from my book what he can bring to it. The dull witted will get dullness and the brilliant may find things in my book I didn't know were there." – *John Steinbeck*

value-added, *adj.* Adding additional features to the product via bundling to entice the customer to buy. "Did I forget to mention that each drone comes with four Hellfire missiles?"

Words That Escaped Me Before My Brain Finished Downloading

valued customer, *n*. Like a new car driven from the showroom, your value is lost the minute you walk out the door with your purchase.

variable, *adj*. Subject to changes. One word that negates any guarantees, warranties, and promises. Valuable word to slip into the contract that requires reading between the lines by people who see it as gibberish. "This ticket guarantees front row seating at the concert subject to variable conditions."

venture capitalists, *n.pl*. New business gamblers.

version, *n*. The other side of the story, though not necessarily the truth either. "That's my customer because I called on him first."

vertical market, *n*. It's a country singer whose market loves country songs; or a philharmonic conductor whose market loves classical music. Each must master the nuances of their skills to match their market in order to establish themselves as experts in their fields. Country singers seem to have much more fun with wilder crowds. Not that classical music patrons can't get wild on occasion. Okay, almost never. But they do get a little giddy-up in their step with the William Tell Overture. Hi-Yo Silver!
  "We'll raise up our glasses against evil forces/ Singing whiskey for my men, beer for my horses." – *Toby Keith*

vetting, *v.t*. Detective work by HR to verify your résumé brags before setting up the interview.
  "What raises a red flag for me are any missing gaps in their timelines of education and employment. That will almost always eliminate them from any further consideration." – *Philadelphia HR manager**

victory lap, *n*. Rubbing it in. "Sorry you lost the promotion. Why don't you join us for drinks as we celebrate mine?"

viral marketing, *n*. Telling your best friend you have 100 Final Four tickets you have to give away by tomorrow.

"Delta Air Lines said it will honor tickets sold at incorrect prices on its website (12/26/13) after customers snapped up bargains like a round trip to Hawaii from North Carolina for $6.90." – *New York Times*

vis-à-vis, *n*. Face-to-face. How people used to communicate in the olden days.

visionary, *n*. Ability to not only see into the future, but to create that future: Thomas Edison, Walt Disney, Steve Jobs.

"You are given a situation. What you are determines what you see; what you see determines what you do." – *Haddon Robinson*

visualize, *v*. Sitting in the aisle seat, eyes closed, jaws clenched, tightly grasping the arm rests, and seeing your plane virtually take off and land safely. It's like a visual prayer. That's what the pilots do as the plane is being pushed back from the gate.

"Only he who can see the invisible can do the impossible." – *Frank Gaines*

voice, *n*. People who have a deeper voice are perceived as having more authority. Not fair, but true.

"When a woman lowers her voice, it's a sign she wants something. When she raises it, it's a sign she didn't get it." – *Unknown*

voicemail, *n*. A chance to leave a good elevator speech that most salespeople blow because they were caught by surprise – again.

"It always scares me when the principal answers the phone. I want to ask them, 'Would you mind hanging up and letting the call go through to your voicemail when I call back?'" – *Seattle commercial real estate salesman**

voicemail menus, *n.pl.* They're like walking through a mine field: make one misstep and you're disconnected. These menus have nothing good to offer.

VP, *n.* Vice President. The title of every bank employee.

waffley, *adj*. Yes. No. Maybe. I don't know.

walk back, *v.t*. When hypocrites and grandstanders try to (insincerely) take back embarrassing or belittling comments they made about others, because they didn't think anyone would call them out on it. They're not taking it back because they know they were wrong – only because they got caught. Politicians are blundering provocateurs of mayhem requiring a parade of walk backs because they have yet to understand that every phone can be used to video record their insults.

"The Park Service should be ashamed of themselves." – *Rep. Randy Neugebauer (R-TX) castigating an innocent park ranger at the World War II Memorial for doing her job and blaming her for the government shutdown that he voted for that included the closure of the memorial (NBC News video, October 3, 2013). After the video went viral and sparked outrage against the congressman, he apologized and tried to walk back his rant.*

walk-in cold call, *n*. Street prospecting for business, often confused with hooking because signs on office doors say "No Solicitors".

"The advantage of a walk-in cold call over a telephone cold call is that you have more than one person's ear. I can't tell you how many sales I've made because someone overheard me talking with the gatekeeper and invited me back to their office." – *Jerry Hocutt*

walking away, *v.t.* An excellent negotiating strategy if you're not getting what you want. If you make it out the door without being stopped, you know you've gone too far.

Wall Street, *n*. Street of Greed.

want, *v*. Bosses want people who *want* to do what others avoid doing and have the attitude that "We can do more, and we can do better."

"I can't want it for him." – *Seattle Mariners manager on returning player who showed up for spring training forty pounds over target weight, showed no desire to participate in offseason conditioning, and was in jeopardy of losing his job*

warm call, *n*. What a sales manager calls a cold call when she's trying to trick her people into making calls to find new business. Only works on rookies who have been selling for less than a day.

warranty, *n*. A promise the product will do as advertised. Should be required on résumés.

water cooler, *n*. What competitors secretly ship to each other to put into their lunch rooms so employees will gather around to gossip and gripe instead of working to defeat them. (Employees would talk about the game last night but they're not allowed to without the "express written consent" of the league.) Circling the water cooler is much better than huddling around the old campfires because there is less smoke to get into your eyes.

WBE, *n.* Women's Business Enterprise. Old girls' network. Much better than the "old boys' network" because they actually work together, compromise, and get things done, instead of making power grabs and talking about how things used to be done.

"Women are the only adults left in Washington. With the federal government at shutdown's door, the 20 female Senate members are setting new standards for civility and bipartisanship. Look out, old boys' club." – *Time Magazine, October 16, 2013*

weasel words, *n. pl.* Answers given to a direct question in order to avoid telling the truth. Any words coming out of a politician's mouth. Any words coming out of a husband's mouth when asked by his wife, "Want to spend Christmas with my folks?" Any words coming out of a wife's mouth before her husband can finish the question, "Hey, wanna...?"

"The more I see, the more I wonder what I'm not seeing." – *Dick Proenneke, Alaska pioneer*

website, *n.* Many start-up business names are dictated by the availability of the website name wanted (which, of course, is already taken).

weekend, *n.* Two days, sometimes three, to get away from work to spend time with your smartphone and tablet. Just another workday.

whale, *n.* The Wall Street (as well as the Las Vegas) dream gambler that's surfacing to be harpooned: spouting a big ego, lots of money, feelings of invincibility, and greed. "Thar she blows!"

"Oh he's not a whale, he's the devil himself!" – *Captain Ahab*

what if. Sales technique to back the prospect into the corner to get a decision. A shakedown to get the answer you want. "What if I told you the offer is no longer good once you walk out the door?"

"What if the hokey-pokey really is what it's all about?" – *Alan Alda*

what you are saying. The customer understood exactly what you said, but is trying to corkscrew it into what he'd rather you would have said, and hopes you don't catch it.

"I know you believe you understand what you think I said. But I am not sure you realize that what you heard is not what I meant." – *Patrick Murray*

whatever it takes. The price you must pay to reach your goal. Determine what you won't do to get it, and then you'll know why you didn't.

"I do want to get rich but I never want to do what there is to do to get rich." – *Gertrude Stein*

what's changed. A good qualifying question to ask when cold calling or networking. New changes indicate new problems and needs. New problems and needs require new solutions.

"Amazon holiday hiring to soar past rivals. 40% increase over 2012. Many of 70,000 temp jobs could lead to long-term jobs." – *Seattle Times, October 2013*

wheeler dealer, *n*. A tough negotiator who can mold compromises in her favor because she has something on you that you want to keep a secret. It's your daughter wanting those flashy new soccer shoes in exchange for not telling dad about your new designer handbag. (He'll never notice the shoes or the purse. He's a man.)

whispering, *v. i*. Whatever is being said, this makes it worse.

whistle blower, *n*. A worker with a conscious who wants to right a wrong. None found in Congress – workers, whistle blowers, or those with a conscious.

wholesale price, *n*. The retailer's price paid to the manufacturer which includes the manufacturer's cost plus profit. By the time the final bill gets to the customer, it looks like an egregious demand in a hostage situation.

"The drug maker charged the hospital $3000 for the vial of medicine which cost it $200 to produce. The hospital then turned around and inflated the price to charge the patient $11,000." – *60 Minutes*

why, *n*. Two of the first questions sales managers should ask of sales applicants: why do you want to sell our service or product? Why do you want to work for us? This should make for shorter interviews.

"He asked me why I was going to law school. Why I wanted to be a lawyer. I didn't have an answer." – *Law school dropout**

"The chief rule of detection is to keep asking 'Why?'" – *Inspector Morse*

WHYDFML, *n*. What Have You Done For Me Lately. Tatoo on every sales manager's forehead.

WIIFM, *n*. What's In It For Me. The first hurdle in getting the appointment.

will, *n*. Determination. The best measure of belief, commitment, and persistence. What competitors try to take away from their competitors.

"All pitchers have the capacity; not all have the determination." – *H.A. Dorfman*

will or would, *n*. Ladies, use either of these two words to get men to do what you want, because they ask for a commitment, not a possibility like "can you" or "could you". That's why men ask, "Will you marry me?" not "Could you marry me?" Sorry men, this doesn't work on women since they don't take words literally like you.

windfall, *n.* Unexpected gain or advantage that catches you by surprise. It's the customer you had written off who calls with a large order on the last day of the month to push you way over your quota.

"If everything is as clear as a bell, and everything is going exactly as planned, you're about to be surprised." – *Unknown*

win-lose, *n.* The voters are celebrating because the recall election threw the bum out.

win-win, *n.* Your ball game just came on TV and your in-laws are leaving.

"How come we never hear father-in-law jokes?" – *Unknown*

wooden nickels, *n.pl.* Political promises.

words, *n.pl.* Characters that matter.

"Taste your words before spitting them out." – *Andrew Card*

words escape me. It's when the brain is stunned with disbelief, the mouth looks like the black gaping entrance to Carlsbad Caverns, and no words are forthcoming. It's the teacher calling to read you your kindergartner's classroom report on "The Funny Things Mommy and Daddy Do At Home."

"I just realized that I don't know why noise comes out of my mouth." – *Dilbert*

workaholic, *n.* Someone who can't identify the scent of a rose.

workload, *n.* Work that seems to increase only for the most competent workers.

"A bus station is where a bus stops. A train station is where a train stops. On my desk I have a work station." – *Steven Wright*

write off, *v.t.* To eliminate an asset from the books as a loss or expense. A passive-aggressive way to say, "You're fired."

wrong, *n.* Like the Supreme Court, something men will never admit to.

"I have never been lost, but I will admit to being confused for several weeks." – *Daniel Boone*

x, *n*. Marks the spot. The line on the contract where customers sign. Make an oversize "X" where the customer signs his autograph, circle it several times, and then point at it with the pen poised for signing. Mesmerizing to the customer and causes him to look and sign without giving it a second thought.

X factor, *n*. A strong but unpredictable influence. Your newest competitor. It's Jan Koum and Brian Acton who applied for a job with Facebook, were rejected, so started their own business WhatsApp in 2009, and sold it to Facebook for $19 billion in 2014.

xyster, *n*. A surgical instrument for scraping bones. Can also be used to scrape you off the ceiling when you find the service department cost you the sale.

"You know that secretary you were rude and dismissive to? That was the boss's wife! Now he wants to see me and he doesn't sound happy." – *Infuriated salesman to service person**

Y

yacht, *n.* The hedge fund manager's bonus paid for with the ROI the investors didn't get. Some are named after candy: "Sucker!" Some are named after secret friends: "The Other Woman". Some are just plain honest: "Stolen".

Yellow Pages, *n.* Landfill.

yes, but. No.

yippee, *interj.* Last workday of the week: "Yippee! It's Friday!" Also the name of really, really tiny peas.

yoga, *n.* What it takes to get from the airplane's window seat to the aisle to hit the lavatory.
 "Surely if God had meant for us to do yoga, He would have put our heads behind our knees." – *Rod Stewart*

you've been served. If you're not hearing this in a restaurant, see you in court.

Z

Zen, *n*. You know what it is, but you can't explain it. Like gas. Or your kids. Or Congress (which acts worse than your kids and gives you gas).
 "Can we cut this Zen crap for a moment?" – *Mari Mancusi*

zero tolerance, *n*. No room for shenanigans. Just another challenge to middle schoolers.

zinger, *n*. The comeback to the customer's snide remark that you have to keep to yourself and can only smile about.
 "Life's tough. It's tougher if you're stupid." – *John Wayne*

zombie, *n*. Brain dead; scary worker going through the motions. One of the 80% of workers accounting for 20% of the work. Who bosses look to replace as soon as they find a "live one".
 "The more I know about people, the more I love zombies." – *J.J. Zep*

Appendix

Wicked Referrals – If You'd Rather Not Cold Call

Give Away Free PDF Abridged Editions and See How Easy It Is to Get Referrals

For a wickedly paltry price you can have your exclusive one-page ad in this PDF abridged edition of *The Wickedly Fun Dictionary of Business* that you can download free to customers, co-workers, friends, and family to increase your referrals. It's the hottest (only?) referral strategy you'll ever have.

referral strategy, *n.* (1) Giving new and current customers a reason to refer you to their friends. (2) A novel promotional idea that's fun, goes viral, and creates a buzz. (3) *The Wickedly Fun Dictionary of Business.*

Its uses are limited only by your imagination.

- ★ Give it to customers to pass on to their other departments and branches to introduce you to their contacts. Use your ad to introduce and cross-sell new services and products.
- ★ Give it away on your social networks.
- ★ Put it on your smartphone and download it when you get customer inquiries, when making sales or service calls, while at networking functions, and when working trade shows.

For details, pricing and your own **free copy**, visit our website below or email **jerry.ht@footinthedoor.com**. Put "Wicked Copy" on the subject line.

www.FootInTheDoor.com

About the Author

nut, *n*. Someone just crazy enough to pull it off.

"When trouble arises and things look bad, there is always one individual who perceives a solution and is willing to take command. Very often, that individual is crazy."

– Unknown

speaker, *n.* Jerry Hocutt

Need a speaker for your next event? Visit Jerry's website or email him at **jerry.ht@footinthedoor.com**.

Learn and laugh. You could do worse. (No. Really. You could. Seriously.)

Just some of Jerry's clients include:

Coldwell Banker · UPS · FedEx · Pepsi Cola · Verizon Wireless · Bank of America · Nextel · Sprint · IBM · Xerox · Coca Cola · ADP · Merrill Lynch · Paine Webber · Office Depot · GE · SBC Communications · Morgan Stanley · Dell · State Farm · Marriott · Hyatt · Ritz-Carlton · Farmers Insurance · U.S. Marines · U.S. Navy · U.S. Army · Clear Channel · Blue Man Group · Chicago Title · MTM Recognition · University of Maryland · Los Angeles Times · Seattle Times · Dallas Morning News · The Press Enterprise · St. Petersburg Times · Key Bank · Wells Fargo Bank · U.S. Bank · Gallup Organization · San Jose State University · Westin Hotels · Hilton Hotels · PEMCO Insurance · New York Life · Allstate · AFLAC · Avaya · First Third Bank · Pre-Paid Legal · Xpedx · Shred-It · Adecco Staffing · LaSalle Bank · Pfizer · Provident Bank · Boeing · Aramark · Motorola · CB Richard Ellis · Johnson & Johnson · Edward Jones · Kinko's · Minolta · Time Warner · U.S. Post Office · Manpower · Staples · Safeco · Wachovia · Condé Nast · Minuteman Press · Staubach · Forest Lawn

www.FootInTheDoor.com

Titles by Jerry Hocutt

Paperbacks and eBooks

Cold Calling for Cowards®: How to Turn the Fear of Rejection into Opportunities, Sales, and Money

Cold Calling Is Like a Colonoscopy Without the Drugs: How You Can Find New Business with Courage, Cold Calling and a Few Less Invasive Techniques

The Book on Sales Tips - one tip, one page, one minute

eBooks Only

The Blueprint for Cold Calling Scripts – What to Say, How to Say It, and Why You Say It

Cold Calling Works? Prove It! – How to Want to Do What You Hate to Do When You Need to Do It

Cast in Stone – 45 Sales Fundamentals That Should Never Be Tampered With

Selling Doesn't Always Have to Be a Struggle – 45 Ways to Put the Fun Back Into Selling

Selling Doesn't Come With Instructions – 45 Ways to Put It Together

Sales Psych – 45 Sales Motivation Tips for Tough Times

Sales Calls Are Auditions – 45 Ways to Get a Callback

Free PDF eBooks available only at www.FootInTheDoor.com

The Wickedly Fun Dictionary of Business – Words That Escaped Me Before My Brain Finished Downloading (abridged edition; includes details for how to use it as a referral strategy for business owners, sales managers, salespeople, and marketing executives)

Lunch? – 20 Sales Questions I've Been Asked Over Lunch

www.ingramcontent.com/pod-product-compliance
Lightning Source LLC
Chambersburg PA
CBHW070734160426
43192CB00009B/1435